Assessment
Tests
for
National 5
Chemistry

D A Buchanan
(Moray House School of Education,
University of Edinburgh)

J R Melrose
(formerly Lenzie Academy)

Published by
Chemcord
Inch Keith
East Kilbride
Glasgow

ISBN 9781870570947

© Buchanan and Melrose, 2014

Printed by Bell and Bain Ltd, Glasgow

Note to teachers / students

This book is designed to cover assessment of all of the essential content of the National 5 Chemistry Course as well as the content of the National 4 Chemistry Course that is judged to be helpful for progression to National 5.

Tests for content of the National 4 Course for which there is no obvious progression to National 5 are also included and indicated with $**$. This content does not have to be revised for the National 5 examination.

Information that may be of use to you can be found in the Data Booklet. A copy of the Data Booklet can be downloaded from the SQA website.
(www.sqa.org.uk/files_ccc/ChemistryDataBookletSQPN5.pdf).

The tests are specifically designed to pin-point areas of difficulty and to check students' understanding of the work covered in the National 5 Chemistry course.

While the tests can be administered to the whole class, it is suggested that they can be more effectively used by students working at their own pace in class, during self-study time in school or as homework. The information from the results of the tests can be used to help students to plan revision. The test results can also be used by teachers / lecturers who are interested in assessing individual or class difficulties.

Each test is, by and large, independent of the others and consequently the tests can be used to fit almost any teaching order.

The variation in length of the tests is a reflection of the different kinds of question which are associated with a particular area of content. Consequently, different allocations of time are required.

Acknowledgement

A number of questions in the exercises come from or have evolved from questions used in Scottish Qualifications Authority (SQA) examinations. The publisher wishes to thank the SQA for permission to use the examination questions in this way.

Index

Test 1   Factors affecting rate

Decide whether each of the following statements is

    A. TRUE   **B.** FALSE.

1. Increasing the temperature increases the rate of reaction.

2. Lumps of calcium carbonate react faster with acid than calcium carbonate powder.

3. A dilute acid usually reacts faster than a concentrated acid.

4. Milk is more likely to turn sour at 0 ^{o}C than at 10 ^{o}C.

5. Small potatoes take longer to cook than large potatoes.

6. Plants grow faster in warm weather than in cold weather.

7. Compared with coal dust, lumps of coal burn very rapidly.

8. Acetylene burns less rapidly in pure oxygen than in air.

9. Chips cook faster in oil at 300 ^{o}C than in oil at 200 ^{o}C.

10. Reactions involving gases go faster when the pressure is increased.

Test 2   Rate graphs

Questions 1 to 5 refer to graphs which show data obtained from reactions of hydrochloric acid.

A.   **B.**

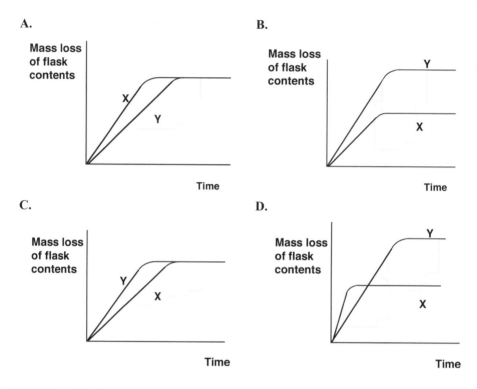

Which graph shows the data likely to be obtained from each of the following pairs of reactions?

Contents of flask X	**Contents of flask Y**
1. 10 g chalk lumps (excess) 50 cm^3 of 1 mol l^{-1} HCl (aq) 20 °C	10 g chalk powder (excess) 50 cm^3 of 1 mol l^{-1} HCl (aq) 20 °C
2. 4 cm magnesium ribbon 50 cm^3 of 2 mol l^{-1} HCl (aq) (excess) 20 °C	4 cm magnesium ribbon 50 cm^3 of 1 mol l^{-1} HCl (aq) (excess) 20 °C

3. 10 g chalk (excess)   10 g chalk (excess)
   50 cm^3 of 0.1 mol l^{-1} HCl (aq)   50 cm^3 of 0.2 mol l^{-1} HCl (aq)
   20 °C   20 °C

4. 4 cm magnesium ribbon   8 cm magnesium ribbon
   50 cm^3 of 2 mol l^{-1} HCl (aq) (excess)   50 cm^3 of 1 mol l^{-1} HCl (aq) (excess)
   20 °C   20 °C

5. 2 g zinc (excess)   2 g zinc (excess)
   50 cm^3 of 1 mol l^{-1} HCl (aq)   50 cm^3 of 1 mol l^{-1} HCl (aq)
   20 °C   40 °C

Questions 6 to 9 refer to four reactions of zinc with excess hydrochloric acid.

Curve **B** was obtained using 1 g zinc powder and 1 mol l^{-1} acid at 20 °C.

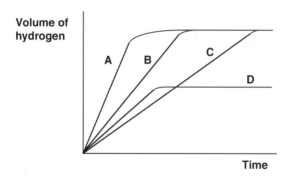

6. Which curve could have been obtained using 1 g zinc powder and
   1 mol l^{-1} acid at 10 °C.

7. Which curve could have been obtained using 0.5 g zinc powder and
   1 mol l^{-1} acid at 20 °C.

8. Which curve could have been obtained using 1 g zinc powder and
   1 mol l^{-1} acid at 30 °C.

9. Which curve could have been obtained using 1 g zinc lumps and
   1 mol l^{-1} acid at 20 °C.

10. The graph opposite shows the volume of hydrogen given off against time when an excess of magnesium ribbon is added to 100 cm³ of hydrochloric acid, concentration 1 mol l⁻¹, at 30 °C.

Volume of hydrogen

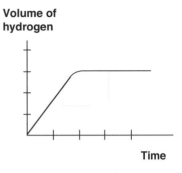

Time

Which graph would show the volume of hydrogen given off when an excess of magnesium ribbon is added to 50 cm³ of hydrochloric acid of the same concentration at 20 °C?

A. Volume

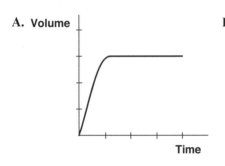

Time

B. Volume

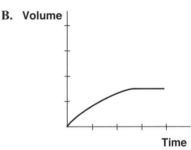

Time

C. Volume

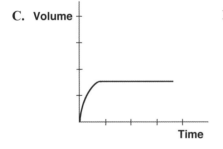

Time

D. Volume

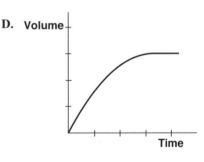

Time

Test 3   Catalysts

In questions 1 to 8, decide whether each of the following statements is

    A. TRUE   **B.** FALSE.

1. A catalyst can increase the rate of a reaction.

2. A catalyst can be recovered chemically unchanged at the end of reaction.

3. A catalyst plays no part in a chemical reaction.

4. Catalytic convertors are fitted to cars to catalyse the conversion of harmful gases to harmless gases.

5. A catalyst is neither a reactant nor a product in a chemical reaction.

6. A catalyst is used up in a chemical reaction.

7. Enzymes can be used in industrial processes.

8. Enzymes catalyse the chemical reactions that take place in living cells.

9. Which graph would best show what happens to the mass of the catalyst as the reaction proceeds?

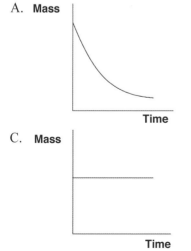

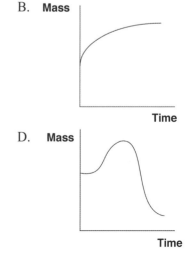

Test 4   Following the course of a reaction

In questions 1 to 8, decide whether each of the following statements is

A.   TRUE   **B.**   FALSE.

1.   The unit for average rate of reaction could be mol l^{-1} s^{-1} .

2.   The unit for average rate of reaction could be cm^{3} s^{-1} .

3.   The unit for average rate of reaction could be mol l^{-1} .

4.   The unit for average rate of reaction could be g s^{-1} .

5.   The unit for average rate of reaction could be g l^{-1} .

6.   For a fixed change in concentration of a reactant, the shorter the time taken, the faster the rate of reaction.

7.   The rate of a reaction is likely to be fastest nearer the end of the reaction.

8.   For some reactions, the reaction rate can double for every temperature rise of 10 $^{\circ}$C.

Questions 9 to 11 refer to the graph which shows data obtained from the reaction of zinc with hydrochloric acid.

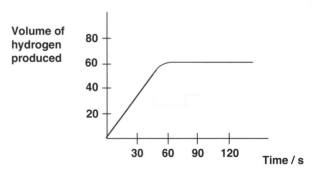

9. What was the total volume of hydrogen produced in the reaction?

    A. $20\,cm^3$ **B.** $40\,cm^3$ **C.** $60\,cm^3$ **D.** $80\,cm^3$

10. How long did it take for the reaction to go to completion?

    A. 30 s   **B.** 60 s   **C.** 90 s   **D.** 120 s

11. What was the average rate at which hydrogen was produced, in $cm^3\,s^{-1}$, in the first 30 s?

    A. 1.2   **B.** 2.4   **C.** 3.6   **D.** 4.8

Questions 12 to 14 refer to the graph which shows how the concentration of a reactant in a reaction varied with time.

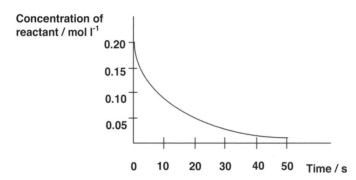

12. What was the initial concentration, in mol l^{-1}, of the reactant?

    A. 0.05   **B.** 0.10   **C.** 0.15   **D.** 0.20

13. What was the average rate at which the reactant was used up, in mol $l^{-1}\,s^{-1}$, in the first 20 s?

    A. 0.0025   **B.** 0.0050   **C.** 0.0075   **D.** 0.0150

14. What was the average rate at which the reactant was used up, in mol $l^{-1}\,s^{-1}$, in the period 20 s to 40 s?

    A. 0.00050   **B.** 0.00150   **C.** 0.00250   **D.** 0.0125

Test 5   About elements

In questions 1 to 12, decide whether each of the following elements is

    A. a metal   **B.** a non-metal.

(You may wish to use the Data Booklet.)

1.	silver	7.	arsenic
2.	sulphur	8.	cobalt
3.	magnesium	9.	mercury
4.	iodine	10.	platinum
5.	aluminium	11.	astatine
6.	sodium	12.	rhodium

In questions 13 to 24, decide whether each of the following elements, at room temperature (20 °C), is

    A. a solid   **B.** a liquid   **C.** a gas.

(You may wish to use the Data Booklet.)

13.	oxygen	19.	chlorine
14.	iodine	20.	bromine
15.	phosphorus	21.	silicon
16.	hydrogen	22.	mercury
17.	calcium	23.	argon
18.	potassium	24.	fluorine

In questions 25 to 36, decide whether each of the following elements is

    A. found naturally as the element

    B. found naturally in compounds but **NOT** as the element

    C. made by scientists.

25. gold

26. americium

27. calcium

28. aluminium

29. fermium

30. silver

31. magnesium

32. sodium

33. zinc

34. californium

35. oxygen

36. chlorine

37. sulphur

38. nitrogen

39. carbon

40. bromine

Test 6   The Periodic Table

1. Approximately how many elements are in the Periodic Table?

    A. 58   **B.** 88   **C.** 118   **D.** 148

2. How many elements in the Periodic Table are noble (inert) gases?

    A. 3   **B.** 6   **C.** 9   **D.** 100

3. Approximately how many metals are in the Periodic Table?

    A. 55   **B.** 75   **C.** 95   **D.** 115

4. If a new element was to be discovered this year, it would most likely be

    A. found in the sea   **B.** found in a rock

    C. made in the laboratory   **D.** found in the atmosphere.

Questions 5 to 8 refer to ways of arranging elements in the Periodic Table.

Decide whether the elements in each of the following lists are in

     A. the same group   **B.** the same period.

5. sodium, potassium, lithium

6. carbon, nitrogen, oxygen

7. phosphorus, aluminium, chlorine

8. chlorine, iodine, fluorine

Questions 9 to 12 refer to chemical properties of elements.

Which element does **not** have similar chemical properties to the others?

9. **A.** neon   **B.** argon   **C.** fluorine   **D.** xenon.

10. **A.** calcium   **B.** aluminium **C.** strontium   **D.** magnesium

11. **A.** chlorine   **B.** astatine   **C.** iodine   **D.** hydrogen

12. **A.** caesium   **B.** potassium **C.** selenium   **D.** rubidium

In questions 13 to 18, decide whether each of the following elements is

     A. stored under oil   **B.** **NOT** stored under oil.

13. gold   16. potassium

14. sodium   17. lithium

15. magnesium   18. aluminium

In questions 19 to 24, decide whether each of the following elements

     A. reacts readily with other substances

     B. does **NOT** react readily with other substances.

19. chlorine   22. helium

20. neon   23. argon

21. calcium   24. sodium

Test 7   Families of elements

The questions in this test refer to families of elements in the Periodic Table.

    A.   the halogens.

    B.   the alkali metals

    C.   the noble (inert) gases

    D.   the transition metals

    E.   none of these

Use a Periodic Table to decide the family to which each of the following elements belongs.

1.	chlorine	11.	platinum
2.	oxygen	12.	fluorine
3.	iron	13.	aluminium
4.	argon	14.	helium
5.	sodium	15.	rubidium
6.	iodine	16.	mercury
7.	magnesium	17.	phosphorus
8.	neon	18.	zinc
9.	copper	19.	xenon
10.	potassium	20.	lead

Test 8   Elements and compounds

In questions 1 to 18, decide whether each of the following substances is

    A. an element   **B.** a compound.

1. Na   7. bromine

2. H_2 8. magnesium nitrate

3. CO   9. sugar

4. HNO_3 10. salt

5. calcium sulphide   11. iron

6. sodium   12. vinegar

In questions 13 to 18, decide whether each of the following lists of substances contains

    A. **only** elements

    B. **only** compounds

    C. **both** elements and compounds.

13. copper sulphide, copper, zinc

14. nitrogen, oxygen, magnesium

15. sodium chloride, lead sulphide, carbon dioxide

16. O_2, Mg, Br_2

17. NaBr, KF, N_2

18. Zn, H_2O, H_2

Test 9   Names of compounds

In questions 1 to 6, name the compounds formed from each of the following pairs of elements.

1. copper and chlorine

2. sodium and oxygen

3. iron and bromine

4. lead and sulphur

5. hydrogen and iodine

6. magnesium and nitrogen

In questions 7 to 18, name the elements in each of the following compounds.

7. hydrogen oxide

8. copper sulphate

9. calcium nitride

10. sodium carbonate

11. nitrogen hydride

12. carbon chloride

13. sodium sulphide

14. calcium sulphite

15. potassium nitrate

16. aluminium bromide

17. sodium phosphate

18. potassium chromate

Test 10 — Particles in the atom

Questions 1 to 5 refer to the atomic particles.

    A. proton   **B.** neutron   **C.** electron

1. Which particle has a positive charge ?

2. Which particle has a negative charge?

3. Which particle is neutral?

4. Which particle does **not** have a mass of 1 amu?

5. Which particle will pass through an electric field without being deflected?

Questions 6 and 7 refer to pairs of atomic particles.

    A. neutrons and electrons   **B.** neutrons and protons

    C. protons and electrons

6. What two particles are found in the nucleus?

7. What two particles are almost totally responsible for the mass of an atom?

8. An atom is neutral because it contains

    A. a number of electrons equal to the sum of the numbers of protons and neutrons

    B. a number of neutrons equal to the sum of the numbers of electrons and protons

    C. a number of electrons equal to the number of protons

    D. a number of protons equal to the number of neutrons.

9.   An atom is made up of 6 protons, 6 electrons and 8 neutrons.

It will have a mass approximately equal to that of

A. 6 protons

B. 12 protons

C. 8 protons

D. 14 protons.

10. An atom is made up of 17 protons, 17 electrons and 18 neutrons.

It will have a mass approximately equal to that of

A. 17 neutrons

B. 34 neutrons

C. 18 neutrons

D. 35 neutrons.

Test 11

Electron arrangement and the Periodic Table

1. Elements in the same group of the Periodic Table have the same

    A. atomic number

    C. number of shells (energy levels)

    B. number of electrons

    D. number of outer electrons.

2. What is the electron arrangement in an atom of calcium?

    A. 2,4   **B.** 2,8,8,2   **C.** 2,1   **D.** 2,8

3. What is the electron arrangement in an atom with an atomic number of 16?

    A. 2,8,8   **B.** 2,8,1   **C.** 2,8,6   **D.** 2,2

Questions 4 to 7 refer to numbers of outer electrons.

    A. 2   **B.** 8   **C.** 4   **D.** 7

What is the number of outer electrons in an atom of each of the following elements?

4. argon

6. magnesium

5. silicon

7. chlorine

Questions 8 to 11 refer to numbers of outer electrons.

    A. 6   **B.** 3   **C.** 1   **D.** 5

What is the number of outer electrons in an atom with each of the following atomic numbers?

8. 8

10. 3

9. 7

11. 13

Questions 12 to 15 refer to the following elements.

A. chlorine **B.** lithium **C.** magnesium **D.** helium

Which element has similar chemical properties to each of the following atoms?

12. an atom with an electron arrangement of 2,8,1

13. an atom with an electron arrangement of 2,8

14. an atom with an atomic number of 9

15. an atom with an atomic number of 20

Question 16 to 19 refer to the electron arrangements shown below.

A. 2,8,7 **B.** 2,8,8,2 **C.** 2,8 **D.** 2,8,1

Which is the electron arrangement in an atom with similar chemical properties to each of the following atoms?

16. an atom with an electron arrangement of 2,8,8,1

17. an atom with an electron arrangement of 2,7

18. an atom with an atomic number of 18

19. an atom with an atomic number of 4

Test 12   Atomic number and mass number

1. What is the atomic number of sodium?

   A. 2   **B.** 11   **C.** 19   **D.** 26

2. All atoms of the one element must have the same

   A. mass number   **B.** number of neutrons

   C. atomic number   **D.** number of particles in the nucleus.

3. The number of protons in an atom is equal to the

   A. mass number   **B.** number of neutrons

   C. number of electrons   **D.** mass number less atomic number.

4. The atomic number of an atom gives the number of

   A. neutrons   **B.** protons

   C. protons and neutrons   **D.** electrons and neutrons.

5. The number of neutrons in an atom is equal to the

   A. number of protons   **B.** number of electrons

   C. mass number less   **D.** atomic number less
   atomic number   mass number.

6. The mass number of an atom is calculated by adding together the number of

   A. protons and electrons   **B.** protons and neutrons

   C. neutrons and electrons   **D.** protons, neutrons and electrons.

7. The number of electrons in an atom is equal to the

   A. atomic number   **B.** mass number

   C. number of neutrons   **D.** mass number less atomic number.

8. An atom of an element has 10 electrons, 12 neutrons and 10 protons.

   What is its mass number?

   A. 12   **B.**   20   **C.** 22   **D.**   32

9. An atom of an element has 92 protons and 151 neutrons.

   What is its atomic number?

   A. 59   B.   92   C. 151   D.   243

10. The number of electrons in an atom is 34 and the mass number is 79.

    What is the number of neutrons in the atom?

    A. 11   **B.**   34   **C.** 45   **D.**   79

11. An atom has 26 protons, 26 electrons and 30 neutrons.

    The atom will have

    A. atomic number 26, mass number 56

    B. atomic number 56, mass number 30

    C. atomic number 30, mass number 26

    D. atomic number 52, mass number 56.

12. An atom has atomic number 20 and mass number of 40.

    The nucleus of this atom contains:

	Protons	**Neutrons**
A.	10	10
B.	20	20
C.	20	40
D.	40	40

13. An atom has atomic number 23 and mass number 51.

    What is the number of electrons in the atom?

    A. 23   **B.** 28   **C.** 51   **D.** 74

14. The symbol $^{238}_{92}U$ shows that this uranium atom contains

    A. 238 protons and 92 electrons

    B. 92 protons and 146 neutrons

    C. 92 protons and 238 neutrons

    D. 146 protons and 92 neutrons.

15. An atom contains 8 protons, 10 neutrons and 8 electrons.

    Which of the following represents the atom?

    A. $^{16}_{8}X$ **B.** $^{18}_{8}X$ **C.** $^{18}_{10}X$ **D.** $^{26}_{10}X$

Question 16 and 17 refer to the information in the table.

Element	W	X	Y	Z
Atomic number	9	19	18	20
Mass number	19	39	40	40

16. Which elements have the same number of electrons?

    A. W and X   **B.** X and Z

    C. Y and Z   **D.** none of these

17. Which elements have the same number of neutrons?

    A. W and X   **B.** X and Z

    C. Y and Z   **D.** none of these

Test 13   Isotopes

1. Isotopes of the same element must have

    A. the same number of protons and neutrons,
            but different numbers of electrons

    B. the same number of protons and electrons,
            but different numbers of neutrons

    C. the same number of neutrons,
            but different numbers of protons and electrons

    D. the same number of protons,
            but different numbers of electrons and neutrons.

2. Some atoms of an element are heavier than other atoms of the same
    element.

    This is because they have different numbers of

    A. neutrons   **B.**   protons   **C.**   nuclei   **D.**   electrons.

3. Which of the following statements is **not** true about isotopes?

    A. Their electron arrangements are the same.

    B. The masses of their nuclei are different.

    C. Their numbers of protons are different.

    D. Their nuclear charges are the same.

4. The two isotopes of carbon, $^{12}_{6}C$ and $^{14}_{6}C$, differ from each other in

    A.   mass number   **B.**   atomic number

    C.   chemical properties   **D.**   electron arrangement.

5. An isotope of oxygen of mass number 18 differs from the most abundant form of oxygen in

    A. the number of atoms per molecule

    B. the number of electrons in the outer shell (energy level)

    C. the number of protons in each nucleus

    D. the ratio of neutrons to protons in the nucleus.

In questions 6 to 11, decide whether each of the following pairs of atoms are

    A. isotopes of the same element

    B. NOT isotopes of the same element.

6. an atom with 6 protons and 8 neutrons
    and
    an atom with 8 protons and 8 neutrons

7. an atom with 10 protons and 10 neutrons
    and
    an atom with 10 protons and 12 neutrons.

8. an atom with atomic number 17 and mass number 35
    and
    an atom with atomic number 17 and mass number 37

9. an atom with atomic number 1 and mass number 2
    and
    an atom with atomic number 2 and mass number 4

10. $^{16}_{8}\text{W}$ and $^{18}_{8}\text{X}$

11. $^{40}_{19}\text{Y}$ and $^{40}_{20}\text{Z}$

12. Which pair or pairs of the following atoms are isotopes of the same element?

$^{86}_{38}W$ $\qquad$ $^{86}_{36}X$ $\qquad$ $^{87}_{38}Y$ $\qquad$ $^{87}_{37}Z$

A. **W, X** only $\qquad$ **B.** **W, Y** only

C. **W, X** and **Y, Z** $\qquad$ **D.** no pair

13.

Atom	Number of protons in nucleus	Nuclear charge
1	50	36
2	50	37
3	49	38
4	52	38

From the information given in the table, which of the following pairs of atoms are isotopes?

A. 1 and 2 $\quad$ **B.** 2 and 3 $\quad$ **C.** 2 and 4 $\quad$ **D.** 3 and 4

14. An isotope of an element can be represented $^{50}_{24}X$.

Which of the following is most likely to represent another isotope of the element?

A. $^{50}_{23}X$ $\qquad$ **B.** $^{52}_{24}X$ $\qquad$ **C.** $^{82}_{24}X$ $\qquad$ **D.** $^{50}_{25}X$

Test 14   Relative atomic mass (atomic weight)

The relative atomic mass of an element is rarely a whole number.

In questions 1 to 5, decide whether each of the following statements is

    A. an explanation of this fact

    B. **NOT** an explanation of this fact.

1.   Different atoms of an element can have different numbers of protons.

2.   It is difficult to isolate pure elements.

3.   Most elements consist of a mixture of isotopes.

4.   Chemical methods of determining the relative atomic masses of elements are inaccurate.

5.   Different atoms of an element can have different numbers of neutrons.

6.   An element consists of two isotopes with mass numbers 40 and 42.

    The relative atomic mass must be

    A. 41 exactly

    B. more than 41

    C. less than 41

    D. between 40 and 42, but impossible to specify.

7. The relative atomic mass of lithium is 6.94.

This is because

A. all lithium atoms have a mass of 6.94 amu

B. most lithium atoms have a mass of 7 amu but a few have a mass of 6 amu

C. most lithium atoms have a mass of 6 amu but a few have a mass of 7 amu.

8. Copper has two isotopes, each with a percentage abundance as shown:

^{63}Cu 75% ^{65}Cu 25%

What is the approximate relative atomic mass of copper?

A. 63   **B.** 63.5   **C.** 64   **D.** 65

9. Neon has two isotopes, each with a percentage abundance as shown:

^{20}Ne 90.5% ^{22}Ne 9.5%

What is the approximate relative atomic mass of neon?

A. 20   **B.** 20.2   **C.** 20.8   **D.** 21

Test 15   Types of bonding

Questions l to 6 refer to types of bonding found in compounds.

    A. ionic   **B.** covalent

Which type of bonding is found in each of the following compounds?

1. sulphur fluoride   4. V_2O_5

2. sodium iodide   5. SiH_4

3. magnesium chloride   6. C_3H_6O

In questions 7 to 12, decide whether each of the following compounds is

    A. made up of molecules   **B.** **NOT** made up of molecules.

7. lithium chloride   10. HF

8. hydrogen oxide   11. K_2CO_3

9. calcium sulphide   12. Al_2O_3

Test 16   Diatomic molecules

In questions 1 to 12 , decide whether each of the following elements

    A. exists as diatomic molecules

    B. does **NOT** exist as diatomic molecules.

1. hydrogen   6. fluorine

2. carbon   7. nitrogen

3. oxygen   8. neon

4. chlorine   9. bromine

5. sulphur   10. iodine

Test 17

Shapes of molecules

Decide on the shape of each of the following molecules.

1. nitrogen hydride

    A.   H—N—H
              |
             H

    B.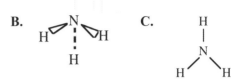

    C.

2. hydrogen oxide

    A.   O
        ⁄ \\
    H   H

    B. H—O—H

    C. H—O
           |
           H

3. carbon fluoride

    A.   F
         |
    F—C—F
         |
         F

    B.

    C.

4. phosphorus hydride

    A.   H—P—H
             |
            H

    B.

    C.

5. carbon dioxide

    A. O=C=O

    B.

    C. O=C
            ||
            O

Test 18

Electron arrangement and ionic compounds (i)

Question 1 to 6 refer to the formation of ions.

    A.   atoms which gain electrons to form ions

    B.   atoms which lose electrons to form ions

    C.   atoms which do not readily form ions

Which statement is likely to apply to each of the following?

1.	an atom with 17 electrons	4.	an atom with 20 electrons
2.	an atom with 10 electrons	5.	an atom with 8 electrons
3.	an atom with 3 electrons	6.	an atom with 2 electrons

Questions 7 to 14 refer to the electron arrangements of atoms and ions.

Decide whether each of the following have

    A.   the **same** electron arrangement

    B.   a **different** electron arrangement.

7.   a magnesium atom and a neon atom

8.   a chloride ion and an argon atom

9.   an oxide ion an a sodium ion

10.   a potassium ion and a chlorine atom

11.   an aluminium ion and a fluoride ion

12.   a calcium ion and an oxide ion

13.   a lithium ion and a fluoride ion

14.   a sodium ion and a neon atom

Test 19   Electron arrangement
                                 and ionic compounds (ii)

Questions 1 to 6 refer to the formation of a calcium ion (Ca^{2+}).

Decide whether each of the following statements is

    A. TRUE   **B.** FALSE.

1. The number of protons increases by two.

2. The number of neutrons remains the same.

3. The number of electrons increases by two.

4. The atomic number remains the same.

5. The mass number decreases by two.

6. The number of electrons decreases by two.

Questions 7 to 11 refer to neon, a gas which is used in lighting and advertising displays.

Decide whether each of the following statements is

    A. TRUE   **B.** FALSE.

7. An atom has the same electron arrangement as a Cl^- ion.

8. An atom has two more electrons than an atom of oxygen.

9. An atom has the same number of outer electrons as an atom of helium.

10. An atom has a stable electron arrangement.

11. An atom has the same number of electrons as an Al^{3+} ion.

Questions 12 to 16 refer to the reaction that occurs when a bromine atom gains one electron to from a bromide ion.

Decide whether each of the following statements is

    A. TRUE   **B.**   FALSE.

12.   The atomic number increases by one.

13.   The particle becomes negatively charged.

14.   The number of electron energy levels increases by one.

15.   The bromide ion has the same electron arrangement as an argon atom.

16.   The mass number increases by one.

17.   A sodium atom and a sodium ion must have different numbers of

    A.   protons, but the same number of electrons

    B.   neutrons, but the same number of electrons

    C.   electrons, but the same number of protons

    D.   neutrons, but the same number of of protons.

18.   A negatively charged particle with electron arrangment 2,8 could be a

    A.   fluorine atom   **B.**   fluoride ion

    C.   sodium atom   **D.**   sodium ion.

19.   The particle with a two-positive charge and an electron arrangement 2,8,8 is a

    A.   calcium atom   **B.**   magnesium atom

    C.   calcium ion   **D.**   magnesium ion.

20. A potassium ion has one more electron than

   A. an argon atom　　　　　　**B.** a calcium ion

   C. a chlorine atom　　　　　**D.** a sulphide ion.

21. In which of the following compounds do both ions present have the electron arrangement of 2,8,8?

   A. potassium chloride　　　　**B.** lithium chloride

   C. sodium fluoride　　　　　**D.** potassium fluoride

22. In which of the following compounds do both ions present have the same electron arrangement as the gas neon.

   A. potassium chloride　　　　**B.** calcium fluoride

   C. magnesium sulphide　　　　**D.** sodium oxide

Test 20

Electron arrangement and ionic compounds (iii)

Questions 1 to 7 refer to types of formulae for compounds in which **X** and **Y** are positive and negative ions respectively.

A. XY **B. XY$_2$** **C. XY$_3$**

D. X$_2$Y **E. X$_3$Y$_2$**

Which is the type of formula for each of the following compounds?

1. aluminium fluoride

2. sodium oxide

3. magnesium sulphide

4. calcium fluoride

5. lithium bromide

6. magnesium nitride

7. barium iodide

Questions 8 to 14 refer to the ratio of positive ions to negative ions in ionic compounds.

A. one to one **B.** one to two **C.** two to one

D. one to three **E.** three to one

What is the ratio of positive ions to negative ions in each of the following compounds?

8. KNO$_3$

9. Na$_2$SO$_4$

10. Na$_3$PO$_4$

11. NH$_4$NO$_3$

12. calcium nitrate

13. ammonium chloride

14. aluminium hydroxide

Test 21   **Molecular representations**

In questions 1 to 10, write the chemical formula for each of the following substances.

1.

2.

3.

4.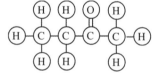

5.

6.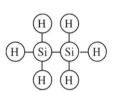

7.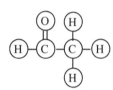

8.

9.

10.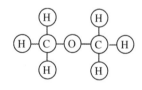

Questions 11 to 19 refer to arrangements of atoms.

A.   B.   C.

D.   E.   F.

G.   H.

11.   Which arrangements represent an element?

12.   Which arrangements represent a substance made up of diatomic molecules?

In questions 13 to 19, decide the possible arrangement for each of the following substances?

13.   hydrogen oxide

14.   carbon tetrachloride

15.   hydrogen chloride

16.   oxygen

17.   phosphorus chloride

18.   nitrogen

19.   chlorine

Test 22   Covalent compounds

In questions 1 to 8, write the formula for the compounds formed from each of the following pairs of elements.

1. hydrogen and oxygen

2. hydrogen and chlorine

3. nitrogen and hydrogen

4. carbon and fluorine

5. phosphorus and chlorine

6. silicon and oxygen

7. selenium and bromine

8. sulphur and iodine

In questions 9 to 14, write the formula for each of the following compounds.

9. nitrogen dioxide

10. carbon monoxide

11. sulphur trioxide

12. carbon tetrabromide

13. carbon dioxide

14. uranium hexafluoride

Test 23   Ionic compounds (i)

Write the formula for each of the following compounds.

1. potassium chloride

2. magnesium bromide

3. calcium oxide

4. sodium sulphide

5. magnesium nitride

6. radium chloride

7. aluminium fluoride

8. aluminium oxide

9. lithium bromide

10. caesium fluoride

Test 24   Ionic compounds (ii)

Write the formula for each of the following compounds.

1. sodium nitrate
2. lithium hydroxide
3. barium sulphate
4. potassium hydrogencarbonate
5. sodium phosphate
6. calcium nitrate
7. potassium hydroxide
8. aluminium sulphate
9. calcium carbonate
10. ammonium chloride
11. magnesium hydroxide
12. calcium hydrogensulphate
13. lithium hydrogencarbonate
14. ammonium phosphate
15. aluminium nitrate
16. sodium carbonate
17. potassium sulphate
18. barium hydroxide
19. ammonium carbonate
20. radium hydrogensulphate

Test 25   Ionic compounds (iii)

Write the formula for each of the following compounds.

1. copper(I) chloride
2. iron(II) oxide
3. iron(III) sulphide
4. copper(II) bromide
5. tin(IV) oxide
6. nickel(II) carbonate
7. lead(II) nitrate
8. iron(II) bromide
9. vanadium(V) oxide
10. cobalt(III) hydroxide

Test 26   **Mixed substances**

Write the symbol or chemical formula for each of the following substances.

1. lithium chloride

2. magnesium nitrate

3. nitrogen

4. potassium hydroxide

5. ammonium bromide

6. rubidium fluoride

7. magnesium sulphate

8. tin

9. sodium sulphide

10. carbon monoxide

11. hydrogen chloride

12. iron(III) chloride

13. calcium

14. bromine

15. strontium chloride

16. ammonium carbonate

17. iron(II) hydroxide

18. hydrogen iodide

19. sulphur trioxide

20. magnesium sulphide

Test 27   Conductivity of elements

Decide whether each of the following elements

    A. conducts electricity   **B.** does **NOT** conduct electricity.

1. zinc solid
2. molten sulphur
3. carbon (graphite) solid
4. molten iron
5. liquid oxygen
6. iodine solid

7. liquid mercury
8. titanium solid
9. argon gas
10. molten lead
11. sodium solid
12. selenium solid

Test 28   Conductivity of compounds

Decide whether each of the following compounds

    A. conducts electricity   **B.** does **NOT** conduct electricity.

1. calcium chloride solid
2. phosphorus pentachloride solid
3. sodium bromide solution
4. copper oxide solid
5. lead iodide melt
6. iron chloride solution
7. liquid ethanol (C_2H_5OH)
8. a solution of sucrose $(C_{12}H_{22}O_{11})$

9. silicon oxide solid
10. carbon dioxide solid
11. magnesium sulphide solid
12. sodium bromide melt
13. liquid hexene (C_6H_{12})
14. solid paraffin wax $(C_{24}H_{50})$
15. a solution of methanol (CH_3OH)

Questions 16 to 21 refer to the table which shows the ability of substances to conduct electricity.

	Solid	Liquid / melt
A.	No	No
B.	No	Yes
C.	Yes	Yes

Which of the above could be applied to each of the following substances?

16. calcium chloride

17. mercury

18. phenol (C_6H_6O)

19. lead

20. sodium bromide

21. octane (C_8H_{18})

Questions 22 and 23 refer to the following substances.

A. iron		**B.** sulphur	
C. lead chloride		**D.** silicon chloride	

22. Which substance does **not** conduct electricity as a solid but does conduct electricity when molten?

23. Which substance conducts electricity **both** as a solid and melt?

Test 29   Different properties

Questions 1 to 5 refer to the table which shows the colour of solutions.

Metal ion	Sulphate	Chloride	Nitrate	Dichromate
X	blue	blue	blue	green
Y	colourless	colourless	colourless	yellow

Decide whether each of the following statements is

    A. TRUE   **B.** FALSE.

1.   The nitrate ion is blue.

2.   Ions of **Y** are yellow.

3.   The dichromate ion is green.

4.   the chloride ion is colourless

5.   Ions of **X** are blue.

Question 6 to 10 refer to the data shown.

Compound	Melting point	Type of bonding
A.	over 500 °C	ionic
B.	over 500 °C	covalent
C.	under 500 °C	covalent

Which set of data is most likely to be true of each of the following compounds?

6.   radium chloride   9.   silicon dioxide

7.   selenium chloride   10. hydrogen sulphide

8.   nickel bromide

Questions 11 to 14 refer to the information in the table.

Substance	Melting point / °C	boiling point / °C	Conduct as	
			a solid	a liquid
A.	963	1560	no	yes
B.	1455	2730	yes	yes
C.	-183	-164	no	no
D.	1700	2230	no	no

11.   Which substance is ionic?

12.   Which substance is a covalent network substance?

13.   Which substance is made up of molecules?

14.   Which substance is a metal?

Test 30 Electrolysis

Questions 1 to 7 refer to the electrolysis of copper chloride solution.

In questions 1 to 3, decide whether each of the following states of copper chloride is

A. suitable for electrolysis

B. **NOT** suitable for electrolysis.

1. solid

2. solution

3. melt

In questions 4 to 7, decide whether each of the following statements is

A. TRUE **B.** FALSE.

4. Copper ions lose electrons at the negative electrode.

5. Copper ions gain electrons at the positive electrode.

6. Chloride ions lose electrons at the positive electrode.

7. Chloride ions gain electrons at the negative electrode.

In questions 8 to 11, decide whether each of the following solutions

A. can be used as an electrolyte

B. can **NOT** be used as an electrolyte.

8. NaBr

9. C_2H_5OH

10. $C_{12}H_{22}O_{11}$

11. $NiCl_2$

Questions 12 and 13 refer to the following substances.

    A.   iodine   **B.**   glucose $(C_6H_{12}O_6)$

    C.   lead   **D.**   sodium bromide

To which substance does each of the following statements apply?

12. When an electric current is passed through the molten substance no decomposition occurs.

13. The passage of an electric current through the molten substance results in decomposition.

Questions 14 and 15 refer to the following experiment.

A crystal is placed on a piece of moist filter paper and a current of electricity passed as shown in the diagram.

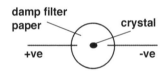

The following compounds were used in the experiment.

    A.   calcium chloride   **B.**   potassium sulphate

    C.   sodium permanganate   **D.**   copper nitrate

14. Which crystal would result in a colour moving towards the positive electrode?

15. Which crystal would result in a colour moving towards the negative electrode?

16. Solid potassium iodide does **not** conduct electricity because

    A. its ions are not free to move

    B. it is a covalent compound

    C. it does not contain enough ions to carry the current

    D. it contains no electrons.

17. A pupil wrote the following statement:

"When an electric current is passed through a solution of ethanol (C_2H_5OH), no decomposition occurs"

This statement is wrong because

    A. decomposition of the ethanol does occur

    B. no appreciable current can flow in the solution

    C. is should be stated that the ethanol breaks up to form ions

    D. ethanol does not dissolve in water.

18. Although solid sodium chloride does not conduct electricity, a solution of the sodium chloride in water carries current because

    A. ions are produced when the current is switched on

    B. ions are produced when the sodium chloride is dissolved in water

    C. water is a good conductor of electricity

    D. ions are freed when the sodium chloride is dissolved in water.

Questions 19 to 23 refer to the electrolysis of copper(II) dichromate solution.

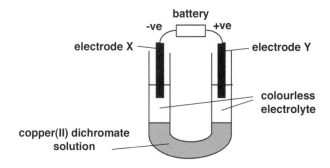

Copper(II) dichromate solution contains blue copper ions and orange dichromate ions.

Decide whether each of the following statements is

A. TRUE **B.** FALSE.

19. Copper forms at electrode **X**.

20. The electrolyte around electrode **X** remains colourless.

21. A blue colour moves to electrode **Y**.

22. Dichromate ions move to electrode **Y**.

23. Electrons move through the solution from **X** to **Y**.

Test 31   Word equations

Write word equations for each of the following reactions.

1. Petrol reacts with oxygen in a car engine to form carbon dioxide and water vapour.

2. In the body, glucose is formed when starch reacts with water.

3. Carbon monoxide burns with a blue flame to form carbon dioxide.

4. Plants make glucose from carbon dioxide and water vapour. Oxygen is released in this reaction.

5. Iron is made in the Blast furnace when iron oxide reacts with carbon monoxide. Carbon dioxide is also formed.

6. Ethene reacts with hydrogen to produce ethane.

7. Silver chloride can be prepared by the reaction of silver nitrate solution with sodium chloride solution. Sodium nitrate solution is also produced in the reaction.

8. Hydrogen peroxide solution decomposes to form water and a gas that relights a glowing splint.

9. When zinc is added to dilute hydrochloric acid, a solution of zinc chloride is formed, along with a gas that burns with a 'pop'.

10. The decomposition of copper carbonate produces copper oxide and a gas that turns lime water milky.

Test 32 Describing reactions

Write a sentence to describe each of the following reactions.

The first one is done for you.

1. $C + O_2 \rightarrow CO_2$
   Carbon reacts with oxygen to form carbon dioxide.

2. $CO + O_2 \rightarrow CO_2$

3. $Zn + Cl_2 \rightarrow ZnCl_2$

4. $Si + Br_2 \rightarrow SiBr_4$

5. $SO_2 + O_2 \rightarrow SO_3$

6. $NH_3 \rightarrow N_2 + H_2$

7. $Na + F_2 \rightarrow NaF$

8. $Fe + S \rightarrow FeS$

9. $CuO + H_2 \rightarrow Cu + H_2O$

10. $AgNO_3\,(aq) + HCl\,(aq) \rightarrow AgCl\,(s) + HNO_3\,(aq)$

11. $Mg + H_2SO_4\,(aq) \rightarrow MgSO_4 + H_2$

12. $CuCO_3 \rightarrow CuO + CO_2$

13. $NH_4Cl + NaOH \rightarrow NaCl + H_2O + NH_3$

14. $Mg + N_2 \rightarrow Mg_3N_2$

15. $K_2CO_3\,(aq) + BaCl_2\,(aq) \rightarrow 2KCl(aq) + BaCO_3\,(s)$

Balance each of the following equations.

1. C + O_2 ➔ CO_2

2. Na + Cl_2 ➔ $NaCl$

3. C + Br_2 ➔ CBr_4

4. C_2H_4 + O_2 ➔ CO_2 + H_2O

5. H_2O_2 ➔ H_2O + O_2

6. Mg + $AgNO_3$ ➔ $Mg(NO_3)_2$ + Ag

7. $NaOH$ + H_2SO_4 ➔ Na_2SO_4 + H_2O

8. $AgNO_3$ + $BaCl_2$ ➔ $Ba(NO_3)_2$ + $AgCl$

9. Na + H_2O ➔ $NaOH$ + H_2

10. Al + Cl_2 ➔ $AlCl_3$

11. KI + H_2O + O_3 ➔ KOH + O_2 + I_2

12. $C_3H_8O_3$ ➔ CO_2 + CH_4 + H_2

13. Al_4C_3 + H_2O ➔ $Al(OH)_3$ + CH_4

14. B_2O_3 + C ➔ B_4C + CO

15. NH_3 + O_2 ➔ NO + H_2O

16. $C_3H_5N_3O_9$ ➔ N_2 + H_2O + CO_2 + O_2

Test 34

Writing balanced equations
- covalent compounds

Use symbols and formulae to write balanced chemical equations for each of the following reactions.

1. carbon   +   oxygen   →   carbon monoxide

2. sulphur dioxide   +   oxygen   →   sulphur trioxide

3. hydrogen chloride   →   hydrogen   +   chlorine

4. hydrogen +   oxygen   →   hydrogen oxide

5. phosphorus   +   chlorine   →   phosphorus chloride

6. silicon   +   fluorine   →   silicon fluoride

7. methane (CH_4)   +   oxygen   →   carbon dioxide   + hydrogen oxide

8. carbon   +   chlorine   →   carbon tetrachloride

9. nitrogen   +   oxygen   →   nitrogen dioxide

10. ammonia (NH_3)   +   oxygen   →   nitrogen   +   hydrogen oxide

11. the burning of sulphur to form sulphur dioxide

12. the reaction of silicon with chlorine

13. the burning of ethene (C_2H_4) to form carbon dioxide and water

14. the formation of hydrogen iodide from its elements

15. the decomposition of nitrogen hydride from its elements

Test 35

Writing balanced equations
- ionic compounds

Use symbols and formulae to write balanced chemical equations for each of the following reactions.

1. magnesium + oxygen ➜ magnesium oxide

2. potassium + chlorine ➜ potassium chloride

3. calcium + dilute sulphuric acid ➜ calcium sulphate + hydrogen

4. magnesium + sulphur dioxide ➜ magnesium oxide + sulphur

5. barium chloride solution + sodium sulphate solution ➜
   sodium chloride solution + barium sulphate solid

6. lithium + dilute hydrochloric acid ➜ lithium chloride + hydrogen

7. sodium carbonate + dilute nitric acid ➜
   sodium nitrate + carbon dioxide + water

8. sodium oxide + dilute sulphuric acid ➜ sodium sulphate + water

9. iron + oxygen ➜ iron(II) oxide

10. calcium + water ➜ calcium hydroxide + hydrogen

11. magnesium hydroxide + dilute nitric acid ➜
    magnesium nitrate + water

12. ammonia + dilute sulphuric acid ➜ ammonium sulphate

13. lead(II) nitrate solution + potassium chloride solution ➜
    lead(II) chloride solid + potassium nitrate solution

14. the formation of lithium chloride from its elements

15. the reaction of aluminium with fluorine

16. the combination of sodium and bromine

17. the burning of aluminium

Test 36

Writing balanced equations - precipitation reactions

(a) Write a word equation for each of the following precipitation reactions.

(b) Use symbols and formulae to write equations.

(c) Balance the equations.

(You may wish to use the Data Booklet.)

1. barium chloride solution and sodium sulphate solution

2. sodium carbonate solution and calcium chloride solution

3. silver(I) nitrate solution and lithium chloride solution

4. lead(II) chloride solution and sodium iodide solution

5. lead(II) nitrate solution and sodium chloride solution

6. sodium hydroxide solution and lead(II) nitrate solution

7. calcium nitrate solution and potassium carbonate solution

8. tin(II) chloride solution and barium hydroxide solution

Relative formula mass

Calculate the relative formula mass for each of the following substances.

1. CO_2

2. Mg_3N_2

3. C_2H_6

4. $CaSO_4$

5. Br_2

6. $Ca(NO_3)_2$

7. $Al(OH)_3$

8. C_3H_6O

9. sulphur dioxide

10. aluminium oxide

11. hydrogen

12. iron(III) hydroxide

13. sodium carbonate

14. ammonium carbonate

15. carbon monoxide

16. sodium phosphate

Test 38

The mole

In questions 1 to 10, calculate the mass of one mole of each of the following substances.

1. NH_4NO_3

2. $Mg(OH)_2$

3. C

4. $(NH_4)_2SO_4$

5. C_2H_5OH

6. magnesium sulphate

7. silicon

8. copper(II) oxide

9. magnesium nitrate

10. calcium hydrogensulphate

In questions 11 to 20, calculate the mass of each of the following substances.

11. 2 mol of Cu

12. 0.1 mol of CO

13. 3 mol of CH_4

14. 1.5 mol of $Ca(OH)_2$

15. 10 mol of O_2

16. 2 mol of sodium sulphate

17. 0.5 mol of iron(II) hydrogensulphate

18. 1 mol of magnesium sulphide

19. 2.5 mol of potassium sulphate

20. 0.4 mol of helium

In questions 21 to 30, calculate the number of moles in each of the following substances.

21. 25 g $CaCO_3$

22. 68 g H_2S

23. 6.4 g S

24. 3.4 g NH_3

25. 8.4 g C_6H_{12}

26. 8.1 g magnesium oxide

27. 80 g sodium hydroxide

28. 1.6 g methane

29. 6.38 g copper(II) sulphate

30. 360 g glucose ($C_6H_{12}O_6$)

Questions 31 to 35 refer to the volume of hydrogen produced from the reaction of metals with excess dilute acid.

The volume of hydrogen produced from one mole of metal is related to the number of moles H^+ (aq) ions that react. The table shows the volumes for three metals under certain conditions.

Metal reacting with acid	Volume of hydrogen produced / litres
Al (s) + 3 mol H^+ (aq)	36
Zn (s) + 2 mol H^+ (aq)	24
Li (s) + 1 mol H^+ (aq)	12

When each of the following reacts with dilute acid under the same conditions, decide whether the volume of hydrogen produced is

A.   12 litres   **B.**   24 litres

C.   36 litres   **D.**   48 litres.

31.   14 g of lithium

32.   9 g of aluminium

33.   23 g of sodium

34.   60 g of calcium

35.   49 g of magnesium

Test 39

Concentration (i)

In questions 1 to 5, calculate the number of moles of solid that must be dissolved to make each of the following solutions.

1. 500 cm^3 of 1 mol l^{-1}

2. 200 cm^3 of 0. 5 mol l^{-1}

3. 100 cm^3 of 0. 1 mol l^{-1}

4. 2 litres of 0.25 mol l^{-1}

5. 200 cm^3 of 2 mol l^{-1}

In questions 6 to 10, calculate the concentration of each of the following solutions.

6. 1 mol of solid dissolved to make 100 cm^3 of solution

7. 2.5 mol of solid dissolved to make 1 litre of solution

8. 0.1 mol of solid dissolved to make 500 cm^3 of solution

9. 0.2 mol of solid dissolved to make 250 cm^3 of solution

10. 0.4 mol of solid dissolved to make 200 cm^3 of solution

In questions 11 to 15, calculate the volume of each of the following solutions.

11. 1 mol l^{-1} solution containing 0.2 mol of dissolved solid

12. 0.5 mol l^{-1} solution containing 1 mol of dissolved solid

13. 2 mol l^{-1} solution containing 0.1 mol of dissolved solid

14. 0.1 mol l^{-1} solution containing 0.5 mol of dissolved solid

15. 0.4 mol l^{-1} solution containing 0.1 mol of dissolved solid

Test 40   Concentration (ii)

In questions 1 to 4, calculate the number of grams of solid required to make each of the following solutions.

1. 50 cm^3 of NaOH (aq), concentration 2 mol l^{-1}

2. 100 cm^3 of KOH (aq), concentration 0.5 mol l^{-1}

3. 1 litre of Na$_2$CO$_3$ (aq), concentration 0.1 mol l^{-1}

4. 25 cm^3 of lithium nitrate solution, concentration 0.2 mol l^{-1}

In questions 5 to 8, calculate the concentration of each of the following solutions.

5. 5.85 g of NaCl dissolved to make 1 litre of solution

6. 1.38 g of K$_2$CO$_3$ dissolved to make 100 cm^3 of solution

7. 8 g of NaOH dissolved to make 250 cm^3 of solution

8. 2.02 g of potassium nitrate dissolved to make 50 cm^3 of solution

9. If 49 g phosphoric acid (formula mass 98) is dissolved in water and the solution made up to 200 cm^3, what is the concentration of the resulting solution?

10. What mass of of pure citric acid (formula mass 210) is required to make 100 cm^3 of solution, concentration 0.2 mol l^{-1}?

11. What mass of pure sodium carbonate (formula mass 106) is needed to make 1 litre of solution, concentration 0.5 mol l^{-1}?

12. If 2.22 g of pure calcium chloride is dissolved in water and the solution made up to 250 cm^3, what is the concentration of the resulting solution?

Test 41   The pH scale (i)

In questions 1 to 4, decide whether each of the following solutions is

     A.   acid   **B.**   neutral   **C.**   alkaline.

1.   a solution with a pH of 8   3.   a solution with a pH of 13

2.   a solution with a pH of 1   4.   a solution with a pH of 7

In questions 5 to 11, decide whether each of the following statements about the pH of solutions is

     A.   TRUE   **B.**   FALSE.

5.   pH 4 is more acidic than pH 6.

6.   pH 8 is more alkaline that pH 10.

7.   pH 3 is less acidic than pH 1.

8.   pH 13 is more alkaline than pH 11.

9.   An acid can have a negative pH.

10.   An alkali can have a pH above 14.

11.   An acid can have a pH of 0.

Questions 12 to 14 refer to the pH of the substances shown in the diagram.

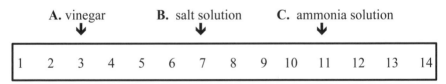

A. vinegar   **B.** salt solution   **C.** ammonia solution

| 1 | 2 | 3 | 4 | 5 | 6 | 7 | 8 | 9 | 10 | 11 | 12 | 13 | 14 |

12.   Which solution would show a decrease in pH when diluted with water?

13.   Which solution would show an increase in pH when diluted with water?

14.   Which solution would **not** show a change in pH when diluted with water?

Questions 15 to 18 refer to samples of rain water, taken as shown.

Water dripping from needles : pH 4.9

Water running down bark : pH 3.8

Rain water collected in clean
beaker away from the tree : pH 5.8

Decide whether each of the following statements is

A. TRUE   **B.** FALSE.

15. The rain water is acidic.

16. The water running down the bark is less acidic than the water dripping from the needles.

17. Pine bark has no effect on the acidity of rain water.

18. Pine needles increase the acidity of rain water.

Questions 19 and 20 refer to coloured solutions made from fruits and flowers.

The colours of these solutions can be affected by pH.

Solution	pH Less than 7	pH 7	pH Greater than 7
A. hydrangea	pink	blue	yellow
B. marigold	orange	orange	orange
C. rose	pink	pink	yellow
D. strawberry	red	red	green

19. Which solution gives a different colour with hydrochloric acid and with sodium chloride solution?

20. Which solution is **not** suitable for showing the difference between an acid and an alkali?

Questions 21 to 25 refer to the pH values of 1 mol l^{-1} solutions of the salts that are shown in the table.

Salt	pH
Iron(III) sulphate	1
Aluminium chloride	3
Zinc sulphate	3
Copper(II) nitrate	3
Sodium chloride	7
Potassium sulphate	7
Sodium carbonate	10
Potassium carbonate	11

By referring to the data in the table, decide whether each of the following statements is

A. TRUE   **B.** FALSE.

21.   The salts are all neutral.

22.   The salts of all the transition metals are acidic.

23.   The sulphate salts are all acidic.

24.   The salts of Group 1 metals are all neutral.

25.   The salts of hydrochloric acid are all neutral.

Test 42   The pH scale (ii)

Decide whether each of the following statements is

    A. TRUE   **B.** FALSE.

1. A solution with pH 2 contains more H^+ (aq) than OH^- (aq).

2. A solution with pH 6 contains a higher concentration of H^+ (aq) than a solution with pH 4.

3. A solution with pH 5 contains H^+ (aq) but no OH^- (aq).

4. A solution with pH 10 contains more OH^- (aq) than H^+ (aq) .

5. A solution with pH 11 contains both OH^- (aq) and H^+ (aq) .

6. A solution with pH 9 contains more OH^- (aq) than pH 11.

7. A solution with pH 6 contains a higher concentration of OH^- (aq) than pH 1.

8. A solution with pH 2 contains the same concentration of OH^- (aq) ions as pure water.

9. A solution with pH 8 contains the same concentration of H^+ (aq) ions as pure water.

10. As the concentration of H^+ (aq) ions in an acid increases, the pH of the solution increases.

11. As the concentration of OH^- (aq) ions in an alkali decreases, the pH of the solution increases.

12. Pure water contains an equal concentration of H^+ (aq) and OH^- (aq).

13. There is a large concentration of H^+ (aq) ions and OH^- (aq) ions in water.

Test 43   Oxides and hydroxides

The questions in this test refer to types of oxides and hydroxides.

    A.   those that dissolve in water to give a solution of pH less than 7

    B.   those that dissolve in water to give a solution of pH greater than 7

    C.   those that do **NOT** have an effect on the pH of water

To which of the categories do each of the following oxides and hydroxides belong?

(You may wish to use the Data Booklet.)

1. sulphur dioxide

2. sodium oxide

3. carbon dioxide

4. copper(II) oxide

5. lithium hydroxide

6. calcium oxide

7. potassium oxide

8. iron(III) oxide

9. phosphorus oxide

10. copper(II) hydroxide

11. nitrogen dioxide

12. barium hydroxide

Test 44   Bases

In questions 1 to 10, decide whether each of the following metal compounds

    A.   can be classified as a base

    B.   can **NOT** be classified as a base.

(You may wish to use the Data Booklet.)

1.	sodium hydroxide	6.	magnesium sulphate
2.	potassium nitrate	7.	lead(II) carbonate
3.	copper(II) oxide	8.	potassium hydroxide
4.	calcium chloride	9.	sodium chloride
5.	calcium oxide	10.	barium oxide

In questions 11 to 20, decide whether each of the following metal compounds

    A.   reacts with water to form an alkali

    B.   does **NOT** react with water to form an alkali.

(You may wish to use the Data Booklet.)

11.	copper(II) nitrate	16.	sodium chloride
12.	potassium oxide	17.	lithium hydroxide
13.	iron(III) hydroxide	18.	lead(II) chloride
14.	barium sulphate	19.	barium hydroxide
15.	copper(II) hydroxide	20.	zinc oxide

Test 45   Salts

In questions 1 to 12, decide whether each of the following compounds

    A. can be classified as a salt

    B. can **NOT** be classified as a salt.

1.	magnesium oxide	7.	hydrogen sulphide
2.	potassium chloride	8.	lithium sulphate
3.	calcium hydroxide	9.	nitrogen chloride
4.	hydrogen chloride	10.	magnesium nitride
5.	sodium sulphate	11.	ammonium sulphate
6.	copper nitrate	12.	silicon oxide

Questions 13 to 15 refer to the following acids.

    A. hydrochloric acid

    B. sulphuric acid

    C. nitric acid

13.   What acid should be used in the reaction with alkali to prepare potassium sulphate?

14.   What acid should be used in the reaction with alkali to prepare sodium chloride?

15.   What acid should be used in the reaction with alkali to prepare lithium nitrate?

In questions 16 to 23, decide whether each of the following reactions

    A.   produces a salt and water only

    B.   produces a salt, water and carbon dioxide gas

    C.   does **NOT** produce a salt and water.

16.   magnesium carbonate with sulphuric acid

17.   copper(II) oxide with sulphuric acid

18.   sodium chloride solution / silver nitrate solution

19.   sodium hydroxide with nitric acid

20.   calcium carbonate with hydrochloric acid

21.   barium oxide with nitric acid

22.   dilute sulphuric acid / barium chloride solution

23.   potassium hydroxide with hydrochloric acid

Test 46   Precipitation reactions

The questions in this test refer to the mixing of pairs of solutions.

Decide whether

      A.   a precipitate is formed

      B.   a precipitate is **NOT** formed.

(You may wish to use the Data Booklet.)

1.   sodium chloride and potassium nitrate

2.   potassium sulphate and barium chloride

3.   lead(II) nitrate and sodium sulphate

4.   calcium chloride and potassium nitrate

5.   sodium nitrate and copper(II) sulphate

6.   magnesium chloride and calcium nitrate

7.   silver nitrate and potassium chloride

8.   ammonium chloride and sodium nitrate

9.   lead(II) nitrate and sodium carbonate

10.   potassium sulphate and copper(II) nitrate

Test 47   Different methods

The questions refer to the preparation of salts by the following methods.

    A. precipitation

    B. reaction of acid with alkali

    C. reaction of acid with insoluble metal oxide

Which method is most suitable for the preparation of each of the following salts?

(You may wish to use the Data Booklet.)

1.   potassium chloride

2.   lead(II) sulphate

3.   iron(III) sulphate

4.   silver chloride

5.   barium sulphate

6.   magnesium nitrate

7.   copper(II) chloride

8.   sodium nitrate

Test 48   Volumetric titrations

1. What volume of hydrochloric acid, concentration $0.1 \, mol \, l^{-1}$, is required to neutralise $100 \, cm^3$ of sodium hydroxide solution, concentration $0.1 \, mol \, l^{-1}$?

2. What volume of sodium hydroxide solution, concentration $0.5 \, mol \, l^{-1}$, will be neutralised by $50 \, cm^3$ of sulphuric acid, concentration $0.2 \, mol \, l^{-1}$?

3. If $100 \, cm^3$ of nitric acid is neutralised by $50 \, cm^3$ of potassium hydroxide solution, concentration $0.2 \, mol \, l^{-1}$, what is the concentration of the acid?

4. What volume of sodium hydroxide solution, concentration $1 \, mol \, l^{-1}$, will be neutralised by $50 \, cm^3$ of hydrochloric acid, concentration $0.5 \, mol \, l^{-1}$?

5. If $20 \, cm^3$ of potassium hydroxide solution is neutralised by $50 \, cm^3$ of sulphuric acid, concentration $0.1 \, mol \, l^{-1}$, what is the concentration of the alkali?

6. What volume of hydrochloric acid, concentration $0.1 \, mol \, l^{-1}$, is required to neutralise $10 \, cm^3$ of potassium hydroxide solution, concentration $0.5 \, mol \, l^{-1}$?

7. If $25 \, cm^3$ of sodium hydroxide solution is neutralised by $14.4 \, cm^3$ of nitric acid, concentration $0.22 \, mol \, l^{-1}$, what is the concentration of the alkali?

8. What volume of sodium hydroxide solution, concentration $0.08 \, mol \, l^{-1}$, will be neutralised by $17.6 \, cm^3$ of sulphuric acid, concentration $0.1 \, mol \, l^{-1}$?

9. What volume of nitric acid, concentration $0.12 \, mol \, l^{-1}$, is required to neutralise $20 \, cm^3$ of potassium hydroxide solution, concentration $0.1 \, mol \, l^{-1}$?

10. If $20 \, cm^3$ of sodium hydroxide solution is neutralised by $15.6 \, cm^3$ of sulphuric acid, concentration $0.1 \, mol \, l^{-1}$, what is the concentration of the alkali?

Test 49   Mixed questions (i)

Question 1 to 5 refer to the information about the atoms shown in the table.

Atom	Atomic number	Mass number
P	22	50
Q	24	50
R	24	54
S	26	54
T	26	56

Decide whether each of the following statements is

    A. TRUE   **B.** FALSE.

1.   Atoms **P** and **Q** have the same number of protons.

2.   Atoms **Q** and **R** have the same number of electrons.

3.   Atoms **P** and **S** have the same number of neutrons.

4.   Atoms **R** and **S** are isotopes of each other.

5.   Atoms **S** and **T** have the same chemical properties.

Questions 6 to 10 refer to magnesium phosphide, a compound that is used to control insects and rodents.

Decide whether each of the following statements is

    A. TRUE   **B.** FALSE.

6.   It has positive and negative ions in the ratio of two to three, respectively.

7.   It contains magnesium, phosphorus and oxygen.

8.   It conducts electricity if it is molten.

9.   It is made up of molecules.

10.   It is solid at room temperature.

Questions 11 and 12 refer to statements which can be applied to elements.

    A.   It is a non-metal.

    B.   It is in the same group as potassium.

    C.   It forms ions with a negative charge.

    D.   It is a solid at 25 °C.

    E.   It has the same number of occupied electron shells (energy levels) as calcium.

    F.   It has the same number of outer electrons as calcium.

11.   Which statement can be applied to **both** gallium and bromine?

12.   Which **two** statements can be applied to **both** strontium and barium?

Questions 13 to 18 refer to radium chloride.

Decide whether each of the following statements is

    A. TRUE   **B.**   FALSE.

13.   The formula is $RaCl_2$.

14.   It is made up of molecules.

15.   It is insoluble in water.

16.   It conducts electricity in the solid state.

17.   The melting point is above 0 °C.

18.   It can be formed by the reaction of radium oxide with dilute hydrochloric acid.

Questions 1 to 5 refer to a solution of citric acid, a solution which is found in oranges and lemons.

Decide whether each of the following statements is

A. TRUE   **B.** FALSE.

1. The solution has a pH of more than 7.

2. The solution conducts electricity.

3. The solution reacts with potassium hydroxide.

4. The solution reacts with sodium carbonate.

5. The solution contains hydrogen ions.

Questions 6 to 11 refer to the reaction of calcium carbonate with dilute nitric acid.

Decide whether each of the following statements is

A. TRUE   **B.** FALSE.

6. The gas produced is hydrogen.

7. The reaction produces calcium nitrate.

8. The same gas will form if the acid used is hydrochloric.

9. The same gas will form if the carbonate used is copper carbonate.

10. The same gas will be produced if calcium oxide is used.

11. The pH of the acid decreases as the reaction proceeds.

Questions 12 and 13 refer to statements which can be applied to solutions.

    A.   It reacts with magnesium oxide.

    B.   It has a pH less than 7.

    C.   It does not conduct electricity.

    D.   It produces chlorine gas when electrolysed.

    E.   The concentration of H^+ (aq) ions in solution is equal to the concentration of OH^-(aq) in solution.

12.   Which **two** statements can be applied to **both** dilute hydrochloric acid and dilute sulphuric acid?

13.   Which statement can be applied to sodium chloride solution but **not** to dilute hydrochloric acid?

Questions 14 to 19 refer to the addition of 20 cm^3 of 1 mol l^{-1} sodium hydroxide solution to 20 cm^3 of 1 mol l^{-1} sulphuric acid.

sodium hydroxide soilution

sulphuric acid

Decide whether each of the following statements is

    A.   TRUE   **B.**   FALSE.

14.   The number of H^+(aq) ions in the beaker increased.

15.   The pH of the solution in the beaker increased.

16.   The number of SO_4^{2-} (aq) ions in the beaker decreased.

17.   Water molecules formed during the reaction.

18.   The final solution contained equal numbers of H^+(aq) and OH^-(aq) ions.

19.   A precipitate was formed.

Questions 20 and 21 refer to statements which can be applied to acids.

    A. Equal numbers of positive and negative ions are present.

    B. A precipitate would be produced with barium hydroxide solution.

    C. The H^+ (aq) ion concentration would decrease when water was added.

    D. Electrolysis would produce hydrogen gas at the negative electrode.

    E. Two moles of sodium hydroxide would be neutralised by one mole of the acid.

20.   Which **two** statements can be applied to **both** dilute sulphuric acid and dilute hydrochloric acid?

21.   Which **two** statements can be applied to dilute sulphuric acid but **not** to dilute hydrochloric acid?

Questions 22 to 27 refer to the addition of water to hydrochloric acid, concentration 2 mol l^{-1}.

Decide whether each of the following statements is

    A. TRUE   **B.** FALSE.

22.   The pH increases.

23.   The acid is neutralised.

24.   The concentration of H^+ (aq) ions increases.

25.   The number of Cl^- (aq) ions in the solution decreases.

26.   The volume of alkali needed for neutralisation decreases.

27.   The speed of the reaction of the acid with magnesium carbonate decreases.

Questions 28 to 34 refer to hydrochloric acid, concentration 2 mol l^{-1}.

Decide whether each of the following statements is

    A. TRUE   **B.** FALSE.

28.   When it is electrolysed, hydrogen is produced at the positive electrode.

29.   It contains more H^+ (aq) ions than Cl^- (aq) ions.

30.   20 cm^3 is neutralised by 10 cm^3 of 2 mol l^{-1} sodium hydroxide solution.

31.   It is produced by dissolving one mole of hydrogen chloride to make 500 cm^3 of solution.

32.   It reacts with copper carbonate.

33.   It does **not** contain OH^- (aq) ions.

34.   It reacts with calcium oxide.

1.   What test is used to distinguish carbon dioxide from other gases?

     A.   It puts out a burning splint.

     B.   It turns lime water milky.

     C.   It turns damp pH paper red.

     D.   It is soluble in water.

2.   When a hydrocarbon burns in a plentiful supply of air, the products are

     A.   carbon and hydrogen

     B.   carbon and water vapour

     C.   carbon dioxide and hydrogen

     D.   carbon dioxide and water vapour.

3.   The presence of carbon monoxide in car exhaust gases is mainly because

     A.   the combustion of the hydrocarbons in the petrol in the engine is incomplete

     B.   the hydrocarbons in petrol form carbon monoxide on complete combustion

     C.   the carbon dioxide produced by complete combustion is changed to carbon monoxide by heat

     D.   some of the hydrocarbons in petrol decompose to form carbon monoxide.

4.   It is inadvisable to burn paraffin in a poorly ventilated room because

   A.   poisonous hydrocarbons are formed

   B.   a mixture of paraffin and air is explosive

   C.   the incomplete combustion of paraffin results in the formation of hydrogen

   D.   a shortage of oxygen may result in the formation of carbon monoxide.

5.   Which compound can be present in car exhaust fumes because of a reaction between the gases in the air?

   A.   carbon monoxide   **B.**   carbon dioxide

   C.   sulphur dioxide   **D.**   nitrogen dioxide

Questions 6 to 9 refer to substances found in exhaust fumes.

Decide whether the presence of each of the following substances is

   A.   a result of incomplete combustion of petrol

   B.   **NOT** a result of incomplete combustion of petrol.

6.   C

7. CO_2

8.   CO

9. C_8H_{18}

10. The oxide of which of the following elements is produced by the burning of some fuels?

   A. chlorine   **B.** phosphorus

   C. silicon   **D.** sulphur

11. In motor cars, air pollution from the combustion of hydrocarbons can be reduced by

   A. the use of catalytic converters

   B. removing nitrogen from the air before combustion

   C. adding a catalyst to the petrol in the engine

   D. increasing the fuel to air ratio.

12. When a sample of gas is burned carbon dioxide is formed.

   The gas **must** be made up of

   A. molecules containing carbon atoms

   B. molecules of hydrocarbons

   C. molecules of carbon monoxide

   D. molecules containing hydrogen atoms.

13. When a sample of gas is burned water is formed.

   The gas **must** be made up of

   A. molecules of hydrocarbons

   B. molecules containing carbon atoms

   C. molecules of hydrogen

   D. molecules containing hydrogen atoms.

14. The products of burning lighter fuel in air are water and carbon dioxide.

    This shows that molecules of lighter fuel contain

    A. carbon atoms and water molecules

    B. hydrogen atoms and carbon dioxide molecules

    C. hydrogen atoms and carbon atoms

    D. water molecules and carbon dioxide molecules.

15. When a cold dry surface was held over a burning fuel, drops of water condensed on it.

    The fuel could contain

    A. carbon monoxide   B. a hydrocarbon

    C. carbon dioxide   D. carbon.

16. When a drop of lime water was held over a burning fuel, the lime water turned milky.

    Which of the following would **not** burn to produce this result?

    A. hydrogen   B. carbon monoxide

    C. a hydrocarbon   D. carbon

Test 2 ***   Fractional distillation

1. The fractional distillation of crude petroleum oil depends on the fact that the different fractions have different

   A. melting points   **B.** boiling points

   C. solubilities   **D.** densities.

2. Which two changes of state occur when petrol is obtained from crude oil?

   A. melting followed by evaporation

   B. condensation followed by by evaporation

   C. evaporation followed by condensation

   D. condensation followed by freezing

Questions 3 to 6 are about uses of the products of fractional distillation of crude oil.

   A. diesel   **B.** bitumen

   C. kerosene   **D.** lubricating oil

3. Which product is used to tar roads?

4. Which product is used as a fuel for jet aeroplanes?

5. Which product is used to reduce friction and wear in car engines?

6. Which product is used as a fuel for trains and certain cars?

Questions 7 to 13 refer to properties of fractions, collected over the temperature ranges shown.

Fraction	Temperature range / ^{o}C
1	Less than 70
2	70 – 140
3	140 – 180
4	180 – 250
5	250 – 350
6	>350

Decide whether each of the following statements about the properties of the fractions is

    A. TRUE   **B.** FALSE.

7.   Fraction 3 is more viscous than fraction 6.

8.   Fraction 2 is more volatile than fraction 4.

9.   Fraction 3 is less flammable than fraction 6.

10.   Fraction 5 is thicker than fraction 3.

11.   Fraction 1 has a higher boiling point than fraction 4.

12.   Fraction 2 burns more easily than fraction 5.

13.   Fraction 3 boils at a lower temperature than fraction 5.

In questions 14 to 20, decide whether each of the following statements about the properties of distillation fractions is

    A. TRUE   **B.** FALSE.

14.   Petrol is more viscous than diesel.

15.   Lubricating oil is more volatile than bitumen.

16.   Diesel is less flammable than the gas fraction.

17. Bitumen is thicker than kerosine.

18. The gas fraction has a higher boiling point than lubricating oil.

19. Petrol burns more easily than diesel.

20. Kerosine boils at a lower temperature than bitumen.

Questions 21 to 26 refer to the following ranges of chain length.

A.	C1 to C4	**B.**	C4 to C12
C.	C9 to C16	**D.**	C15 to C25
E.	C20 to C70	**F.**	greater than C70

Decide which range is typical of the molecules found in each of the following fractions.

21. petrol

22. bitumen

23. kerosine

24. the gas fraction

25. lubricating oil

26. diesel

Test 3   Structure of hydrocarbons

In questions 1 to 12, decide whether each of the hydrocarbons is

    A.   a straight-chain alkane   **B.**   a cycloalkane

    C.   an alkene   **D.**   saturated   **E.**   unsaturated.

(Note that for each question, TWO responses should be given.)

1.   ethane

2.   cyclopropane

3.   propene

4.   cyclopentane

5.   heptane

6.   octene

7.

```
     H
     |
 H—C—H
     |
     H
```

8.

```
H             H
 \           /
  C = C
 /           \
H             H
```

9.

```
 H   H
 |   |
H—C—C—H
 |   |
H—C—C—H
 |   |
 H   H
```

10.

```
      H    H
       \  /
        C
  H    / \    H
   \  /   \  /
  H—C     C—H
  H—C     C—H
   /  \   /  \
  H    \ /    H
        C
       / \
      H   H
```

11.

```
 H  H  H  H  H
 |  |  |  |  |
H—C—C—C—C—C—H
 |  |  |  |  |
 H  H  H  H  H
```

12.

```
H              H  H  H
 \             |  |  |
  C = C—C—C—C—H
 /             |  |  |
H       H      H  H  H
```

Questions 13 to 18 refer to the structure of hydrocarbons.

A.

$$H-\overset{\overset{\displaystyle H}{|}}{\underset{\underset{\displaystyle H}{|}}{C}}-H$$

B.

$$H-\overset{\overset{\displaystyle H}{|}}{\underset{\underset{\displaystyle H}{|}}{C}}-\overset{\overset{\displaystyle H}{|}}{\underset{\underset{\displaystyle H}{|}}{C}}-H$$

C.

$$\underset{H}{\overset{H}{>}}C=C\underset{H}{\overset{H}{<}}$$

D.

$$H-\overset{\overset{\displaystyle H}{|}}{\underset{\underset{\displaystyle H}{|}}{C}}-\overset{\overset{\displaystyle H}{|}}{\underset{\underset{\displaystyle H}{|}}{C}}-\overset{\overset{\displaystyle H}{|}}{\underset{\underset{\displaystyle H}{|}}{C}}-H$$

E.

$$\underset{H}{\overset{H}{>}}C=\overset{\overset{\displaystyle H}{|}}{\underset{\underset{\displaystyle H}{|}}{C}}-\overset{\overset{\displaystyle H}{|}}{\underset{\underset{\displaystyle H}{|}}{C}}-H$$

F.

$$\underset{H}{\overset{H}{>}}C\underset{H}{\overset{H}{<}}$$ ... triangle ring

G.

$$H-\overset{\overset{\displaystyle H}{|}}{\underset{\underset{\displaystyle H}{|}}{C}}-\overset{\overset{\displaystyle H}{|}}{\underset{\underset{\displaystyle H}{|}}{C}}-\overset{\overset{\displaystyle H}{|}}{\underset{\underset{\displaystyle H}{|}}{C}}-\overset{\overset{\displaystyle H}{|}}{\underset{\underset{\displaystyle H}{|}}{C}}-H$$

H.

$$\underset{H}{\overset{H}{>}}C=\overset{\overset{\displaystyle H}{|}}{\underset{\underset{\displaystyle H}{|}}{C}}-\overset{\overset{\displaystyle H}{|}}{\underset{\underset{\displaystyle H}{|}}{C}}-\overset{\overset{\displaystyle H}{|}}{\underset{\underset{\displaystyle H}{|}}{C}}-H$$

I.

$$H-\overset{\overset{\displaystyle H}{|}}{\underset{\underset{\displaystyle H}{|}}{C}}-\overset{\overset{\displaystyle H}{|}}{C}=\overset{\overset{\displaystyle H}{|}}{C}-\overset{\overset{\displaystyle H}{|}}{\underset{\underset{\displaystyle H}{|}}{C}}-H$$

J.

$$H-\overset{\overset{\displaystyle H}{|}}{\underset{\underset{\displaystyle H}{|}}{C}}-\overset{\overset{\displaystyle H}{|}}{\underset{\underset{\displaystyle H}{|}}{C}}-H$$
$$H-\overset{\overset{\displaystyle H}{|}}{\underset{\underset{\displaystyle H}{|}}{C}}-\overset{\overset{\displaystyle H}{|}}{\underset{\underset{\displaystyle H}{|}}{C}}-H$$

13.   What is the structure of butane?

14.   What is the structure of but-1-ene?

15.   What is the structure of cyclopropane?

16.   What is the structure of ethene?

17.   What is the structure of methane?

18.   What is the structure of propene?

Test 4   Homologous series

In questions 1 to 4, decide whether each of the following hydrocarbons is

    A.   an alkane   **B.**   an alkene.

1. C_3H_8

2. C_2H_4

3. $C_{20}H_{42}$

4. $C_{16}H_{32}$ (straight-chain)

Questions 5 to 10 refer to the following molecular formulae for hydrocarbons.

    A. C_5H_{10} **B.** C_5H_{12} **C.** C_6H_{12} **D.** C_6H_{14}

What is the molecular formula for each of the following hydrocarbons?

5.   hexane

6.   pentene

7.   cyclohexane

8.   pentane

9.   hexene

10.   cyclopentane

11.   How many hydrogen atoms are in a straight-chain alkane with 25 carbon atoms?

     A.   48   **B.**   50   **C.**   52   **D.**   54

12. How many hydrogen atoms are in a straight-chain alkene with 12 carbon atoms?

    A. 20   **B.** 22   **C.** 24   **D.** 26

13. How many hydrogen atoms are in a cycloalkane with 16 carbon atoms?

    A. 28   **B.** 30   **C.** 32   **D.** 34

14. How many hydrogen atoms are in a cycloalkene with 21 carbon atoms?

    A. 40   **B.** 42   **C.** 44   **D.** 46

15. Which of the following could **not** be either a straight-chain alkane or a cycloalkane?

    A. C_4H_{10} **B.** C_5H_{10} **C.** C_6H_{12} **D.** C_7H_{12}

In questions 16 to 20, decide which hydrocarbon is **not** a member of the same homologous series as the others.

16. **A.** ethene   **B.** hexene   **C.** butene   **D.** cyclopropane

17. **A.** butane   **B.** ethene   **C.** methane   **D.** propane

18. **A.** C_3H_8 **B.** C_5H_{12} **C.** C_6H_{12} **D.** C_7H_{16}

19. **A.** CH_4 **B.** C_3H_6 **C.** C_6H_{12} **D.** C_8H_{16}

20. Hydrocarbons with a formula mass of :

    A. 16   **B.** 44   **C.** 84   **D.** 100

21. Which hydrocarbon is a member of the same homologous series as the compound represented by the formula C_4H_{10}?

A. 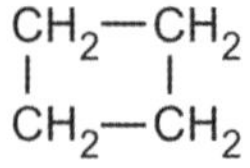 $CH_2\text{—}CH_2$
$\quad\ \ CH_2\text{—}CH_2$

B. $CH_3\text{—}CH\text{=}CH_2$

C. $CH_2\text{=}CH_2$

D. CH_4

22. Which compound has the general formula $C_nH_{2n}O$?

A.

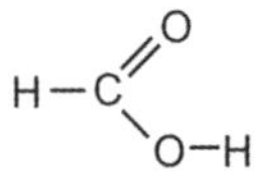

B.

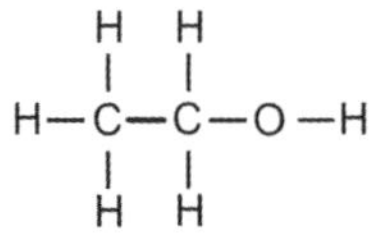

C.

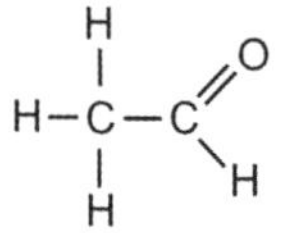

D.

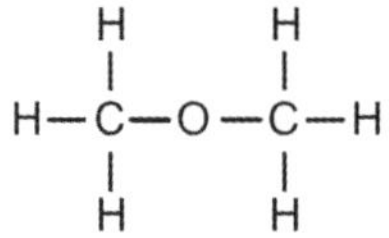

23. Which compound belongs to a series with the general formula $C_nH_{2n}S$?

A. $CH_3\text{—}S\text{—}CH_3$

B. $CH_3\text{—}S\text{—}C_2H_5$

C.

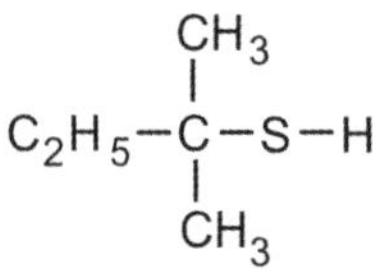

D.

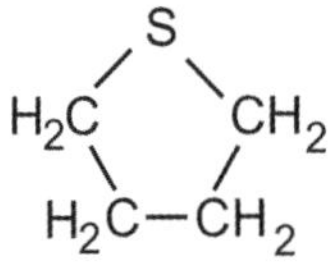

Test 5   Systematic naming of hydrocarbons

Write the systematic name for each of the following hydrocarbons.

1.

$$CH_3-\underset{\underset{H}{|}}{\overset{\overset{CH_3}{|}}{C}}-\underset{\underset{H}{|}}{\overset{\overset{CH_3}{|}}{C}}-CH_3$$

7.

$$CH_3-CH_2-\underset{\underset{H}{|}}{\overset{\overset{CH_3}{|}\\\overset{|}{CH_2}}{C}}-CH_2-CH_3$$

2. $CH_2{=}CH-CH_2-CH_2-CH_3$

8.

$$CH_3-\underset{\underset{H}{|}}{\overset{\overset{CH_3}{|}}{C}}-CH_2-CH{=}CH_2$$

3.

$$CH_3-\overset{\overset{H}{|}}{C}{=}\overset{\overset{H}{|}}{C}-\underset{\underset{H}{|}}{\overset{\overset{CH_3}{|}}{C}}-CH_3$$

9.

$$CH_3-CH_2-\underset{\underset{CH_3}{|}}{\overset{\overset{CH_3}{|}}{C}}-CH_3$$

4.

$$H-\underset{\underset{CH_3}{|}}{\overset{\overset{CH_3}{|}}{C}}-CH_2-CH_2-CH_3$$

10.

$$CH_3-\underset{\underset{H}{|}}{\overset{\overset{CH_3}{|}\\\overset{|}{CH_2}}{C}}-CH_2-CH_3$$

5.

$$CH_3-\overset{\overset{\overset{H\diagdown \diagup H}{C}}{\|}}{C}-CH_2-CH_3$$

11.

$$\begin{array}{c}H\diagdown\quad CH_2\\ \quad C\diagup \quad \diagdown CH_2\\ \|\quad\quad\quad |\\ \quad C\diagdown\quad CH_2\\ H\diagup\quad CH_2\end{array}$$

6.

$$CH_3-\overset{\overset{H}{|}}{C}{=}\underset{\underset{CH_3}{|}}{C}-\underset{\underset{H}{|}}{\overset{\overset{CH_3}{|}}{C}}-CH_3$$

12.

$$\begin{array}{c}CH_2\\ H_2C\diagup\quad \diagdown CH_2\\ |\quad\quad\quad\quad |\\ H_2C\diagdown\quad \diagup CH_2\\ C\\ H\diagup\quad \diagdown CH_3\end{array}$$

Test 6

Decide whether each of the following pairs of compounds are

    A. isomers   **B.**   **NOT** isomers.

1. $CH_3-CH_2-CH_2-CH_3$ and CH_3-CH_2
                                                                 CH_2-CH_3

2. CH_3
          |
   $CH_3-CH-CH_3$ and $CH_3-CH_2-CH_2-CH_3$

3. $CH_3-CH-CH_3$ and CH_3
               |
             CH_3 $CH_3-CH-CH_3$

4. $CH_3-CH_2-CH_3$ and $CH_2=CH-CH_3$

5. $CH_3-CH_2-CH_3$ and CH_3-CH_3

6. $CH_3-CH_2-CH_2-CH_2-CH_3$ and CH_3
                                                      |
                                               $CH_3-CH-CH_2-CH_3$

7. CH_3 and $CH_3-CH_2-CH-CH_3$
       |
   $CH_3-CH-CH_2-CH_3$ CH_3

8. $CH_3-CH_2-CH_2-CH_2-CH_3$ and CH_3
                                                     |
                                           CH_3-C-CH_3
                                                    |
                                           CH_3

9. CH_3 and
       |
   $CH_3-CH-CH_2-CH_3$ CH_3
                                                    |
                                         CH_3-C-CH_3
                                                    |
                                           CH_3

10.
$$CH_3-\overset{\overset{\displaystyle CH_3}{|}}{CH}-CH_2-CH_3$$

and

$$CH_3-CH_2-\overset{\overset{\displaystyle CH_3}{|}}{CH}-CH_3$$

11. $CH_3-CH_2-CH_2-CH_2-CH_3$

and

$$\overset{\overset{\displaystyle CH_3}{|}}{CH_2}-CH_2-\overset{\underset{\displaystyle CH_3}{|}}{CH_2}$$

12. $CH_2{=}CH-CH_2-CH_3$

and

$CH_3-CH_2-CH{=}CH_2$

13. $CH_2{=}CH-CH_2-CH_3$

and

$CH_3-CH{=}CH-CH_3$

14. $CH_2{=}CH-CH_2-CH_3$

and

$$\begin{array}{c} CH_2-CH_2 \\ |\quad\quad| \\ CH_2-CH_2 \end{array}$$

15. $CH_3-CH_2-CH_2-CH_3$

and

$$\begin{array}{c} CH_2-CH_2 \\ |\quad\quad| \\ CH_2-CH_2 \end{array}$$

16. $CH_3-CH_2-CH_2-CH_3$

and

$$CH_3-\overset{\overset{\displaystyle CH_3}{|}}{C}{=}CH-CH_3$$

17.
$$CH_2{=}\overset{\overset{\displaystyle CH_3}{|}}{C}-CH_2-CH_3$$

and

$$CH_3-\overset{\overset{\displaystyle CH_3}{|}}{C}{=}CH-CH_3$$

18. 2-methylpentane   and   heptane

19. 2,3-dimethylbutane   and   hexane

20. 2-methylpent-1-ene   and   hex-1-ene

21. methylpropane   and   butane

22. but-2-ene   and   2-methylbut-1-ene

Test 7 ***   Cracking of hydrocarbons

Questions 1 to 10 refer to the experiment shown.

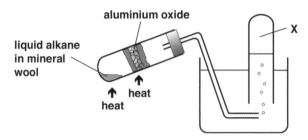

In the apparatus, the mineral wool was soaked with a liquid alkane, $C_{12}H_{26}$. Its vapour was passed over hot aluminium oxide and gas(es) collected at **X** by displacement of water.

Decide whether each of the statements is

      A. TRUE   **B.**   FALSE.

1.   Some of the gases formed are not hydrocarbons.

2.   The aluminium oxide acts as a catalyst.

3.   Only methane gas is produced.

4.   The gases collected quickly decolourises bromine.

5.   The gases collected **could** contain ethene.

6.   The gases collected contains saturated molecules.

7.   The gases collected contains a mixture of hydrocarbons.

8.   The gases collected contains unsaturated molecules.

9.   Molecules with the formula $C_{13}H_{26}$ are found in the gases .

10.   The gas collected **could** contain ethane.

11. $C_{16}H_{34}$ ➔ $C_{10}H_{20}$ + **X**

What is the formula for **X**?

A. C_6H_{14} **B.** $C_{10}H_{22}$ **C.** $C_{16}H_{12}$ **D.** $C_{26}H_{24}$

12. $C_{10}H_{22}$ ➔ C_6H_{12} + C_2H_6 + **Y**

Y must be

A. methane   **B.** ethene   **C.** butane   **D.** butene.

13. Hexane can be cracked to give ethene and another hydrocarbon.

The other hydrocarbon must be

A. propane   **B.** propene   **C.** butane   **D.** butene.

14. A C_{11} alkane is cracked into pentane and two other straight-chain hydrocarbons.

If one of these is ethene, the other must be

A. propane   **B.** propene   **C.** butane   **D.** butene.

15. Which equation shows an industrial cracking process?

A. $CH_3 - CH_2 - CH_2 - CH_2 - CH_3$ ➔ $CH_3 - CH_2 - CH_3 + CH_2 = CH_2$

B. $CH_3 - CH = CH_2$ ➔ $CH_3 - CH_2 - CH_3$

C. $CH_3 - CH_2 - CH_2 - CH_2 - CH_3$ ➔ $CH_3 - \overset{\overset{\displaystyle CH_3}{|}}{CH} - CH_2 - CH_3$

Test 8

Addition reactions

In questions 1 to 12, decide whether each of the following hydrocarbons

    A.   reacts quickly with bromine

    B.   does **NOT** react quickly with bromine.

1. propane

2. propene

3. cyclopropane

4. cyclopentene

5.

$$H-\overset{\displaystyle H}{\underset{\displaystyle H}{C}}-\overset{\displaystyle H}{\underset{\displaystyle H}{C}}-\overset{\displaystyle H}{\underset{\displaystyle H}{C}}-\overset{\displaystyle H}{\underset{\displaystyle H}{C}}-H$$

6.

$$H-\overset{\displaystyle H}{\underset{\displaystyle H}{C}}-\overset{\displaystyle H}{\underset{\displaystyle H}{C}}-\overset{\displaystyle H}{C}=C\overset{\displaystyle H}{\underset{\displaystyle H}{}}$$

7.

$$\begin{array}{c} H-\overset{\displaystyle H}{C}-\overset{\displaystyle H}{C}-H \\ H-\overset{\displaystyle }{C}-\overset{\displaystyle }{C}-H \\ \overset{\displaystyle H}{} \overset{\displaystyle H}{} \end{array}$$

8.

9. C_2H_4

10. CH_4

11. C_6H_{12} (cyclo)

12. C_5H_{12}

In questions 13 to 18, decide whether each of the following carbon compounds

    A. could be a product of the reaction between ethene and bromine

    B. could **NOT** be a product of the reaction between ethene and bromine.

13.
```
    H  H
    |  |
H — C— C— Br
    |  |
    Br H
```

16.
```
    H  Br
    |  |
H — C— C— H
    |  |
    Br H
```

14.
```
    H  H
    |  |
H — C— C— H
    |  |
    Br Br
```

17.
```
    H  Br
    |  |
H — C— C— Br
    |  |
    H  H
```

15.
```
    Br H
    |  |
H — C— C— H
    |  |
    Br H
```

18.
```
     H  H
     |  |
Br — C— C— Br
     |  |
     H  H
```

In questions 19 to 24, decide whether each of the following carbon compounds

    A. could be a product of the reaction between propene and bromine.

    B. could **NOT** be a product of the reaction between propene and bromine.

19.
```
    H  H  H
    |  |  |
H — C— C— C— H
    |  |  |
    Br H  Br
```

22.
```
    H  Br H
    |  |  |
H — C— C— C— Br
    |  |  |
    H  H  H
```

20.
```
    Br H  H
    |  |  |
H — C— C— C— H
    |  |  |
    H  Br H
```

23.
```
    H  H  H
    |  |  |
H — C— C— C— H
    |  |  |
    Br Br H
```

21.
```
     H  H  H
     |  |  |
Br — C— C— C— Br
     |  |  |
     H  H  H
```

24.
```
     Br H  H
     |  |  |
Br — C— C— C— H
     |  |  |
     H  H  H
```

25. A hydrocarbon, molecular formula C_5H_{10}, does **not** quickly decolourise bromine.

Which hydrocarbon could it be?

    A. pentane   **B.** cyclopentane

    C. pentene   **D.** cyclopentene

26. When a molecule of the compound $CH_2 = CH – CH = CH_2$ completely reacts with bromine, the number of molecules of bromine used would be

    A. 1   **B.** 2   **C.** 3   **D.** 4.

27. What is formed when butene reacts with hydrogen?

    A. ethane   **B.** propane   **C.** butane   **D.** hexane

28. What hydrocarbon reacts with hydrogen to form hexane?

    A. propene   **B.** pentane   **C.** hexene   **D.** octane

In questions 29 to 32, decide whether each of the following reactions is

    A. an addition reaction

    B. **NOT** an addition reaction.

29. $CH_3 – CH_2 – CH_2 – CH_2 – CH_3 \rightarrow CH_3 – CH_2 – CH_3 + CH_2 = CH_2$

30. $CH_3 – CH = CH_2 \rightarrow CH_3 – CH_2 – CH_3$

31. $CH_3 – CH_2 – CH_2 – CH_2 – CH_3 \rightarrow CH_3 – \overset{\overset{\displaystyle CH_3}{|}}{C}H – CH_2 – CH_3$

32. $CH_4 + 3O_2 \rightarrow 2CO_2 + 2H_2O$

Test 9 ***   Carbohydrates

1. Which element is **not** contained in a carbohydrate.

    A. hydrogen   **B.** carbon

    C. nitrogen   **D.** oxygen

In questions 2 to 7, decide whether each of the following substances

    A. can be classified as a carbohydrate

    B. can **NOT** be classified as a carbohydrate.

2. $C_{12}H_{22}O_{11}$ 5. H_2O_2

3. C_6H_{14} 6. C_2H_6O

4. $C_6H_{12}O_6$ 7. $C_3H_6O_2$

Questions 8 and 9 refer to solutions.

    A. salt solution   **B.** iodine solution

    C. Benedict's solution   **D.** bromine solution

8. What solution is used to test for starch?

9. What solution is used to test for glucose?

Questions 10 and 11 refer to colours.

    A. brick red **B.** sky blue **C.** blue/black **D.** green/blue

10. What colour is produced when the test for glucose is positive?

11. What colour is produced when the test for starch is positive?

Test 10 ***　　　　　Reactions of carbohydrates

Decide whether each of the following statements is

　　　　A. TRUE　　　　　　　　**B.** FALSE.

1. Glucose molecules are small compared to starch molecules.

2. The joining up of glucose molecules to form starch is an example of a polymerisation reaction.

3. Plants convert glucose into starch for storing energy.

4. Glucose is the monomer used to build up starch.

5. Glucose breaks down to form starch during digestion.

6. Polymerisation of glucose takes place in plants.

7. Glucose molecules are small enough to pass through the gut wall.

8. Enzymes play a part in the digestion of starch.

9. The breakdown of starch using saliva is best carried out at room temperature.

10. Between 40 °C and 60 °C, body enzymes become more effective as the temperature increases.

11. Carbon dioxide is produced when glucose molecules join up to make starch.

12. Starch molecules break down by reacting with water molecules.

Test 11 ***   Alcohol

Decide whether each of the following statements is

      A. TRUE   **B.** FALSE.

1.   Alcoholic drinks can be made from fruit or vegetables.

2.   Yeast is required for making alcohol by fermentation.

3.   Alcohol is produced from carbohydrates by an addition reaction.

4.   A biological catalyst is called an enzyme.

5.   Oxygen gas is used up in the making of alcohol from carbohydrates.

6.   Distillation is a method of increasing the alcohol concentration in alcoholic drinks.

7.   Alcohol is a sedative and slows down the nervous system.

8.   Fermentation is a way of separating alcohol and water.

9.   Carbon dioxide gas is produced in the making of alcohol from carbohydrates.

10.   Glucose can be used to make alcohol .

11.   Fermentation is a way of separating liquids due to a difference in boiling point.

12.   Whisky (40% alcohol) is made by fermentation followed by distillation.

13.   The manufacture of beer (5% alcohol) involves distillation.

14.   At high concentrations, alcohol can destroy the enzyme responsible for fermentation of glucose.

Test 12

Structures of alcohols, carboxylic acids and esters

The questions in this test refer to oxygen-containing organic compounds.

A.

$$CH_3-\overset{\overset{\displaystyle O}{\|}}{C}-CH_3$$

B.

$$CH_3-C\overset{\displaystyle O}{\underset{\displaystyle OH}{<}}$$

C. CH_3-OH

D.

$$CH_3-CH_2-C\overset{\displaystyle O}{\underset{\displaystyle O-CH_3}{<}}$$

E.

$$CH_3-O\overset{\displaystyle O}{\underset{}{\diagdown}}C-H$$

F.

$$CH_3-\overset{\overset{\displaystyle H}{|}}{\underset{\underset{\displaystyle OH}{|}}{C}}-CH_3$$

G.

$$H-C\overset{\displaystyle O}{\underset{\displaystyle OH}{<}}$$

H.

$$CH_3-O\overset{\displaystyle O}{\underset{}{\diagdown}}C-CH_3$$

I.

$$CH_3-CH_2-C\overset{\displaystyle O}{\underset{\displaystyle H}{<}}$$

J. $CH_3-O-CH_2-CH_3$

K. CH_3-CH_2-COOH

L. CH_3-CH_2OH

1. Pick out **all** the compounds which are **alcohols**.

2. Pick out **all** the compounds which are **carboxylic acids**.

3. Pick out **all** the compounds which are **esters**.

Test 13

In questions 1 to 6, name each of the following carbon compounds.

1. CH_3-OH

4. $H-C\begin{smallmatrix}O\\OH\end{smallmatrix}$ (H—C, double bond O, —OH)

2. $CH_3-C\begin{smallmatrix}O\\OH\end{smallmatrix}$ (CH₃—C, double bond O, —OH)

5. CH_3-CH_2-OH

3. $CH_3-CH_2-CH_2-OH$

6. $CH_3-CH_2-CH_2-COOH$

Questions 7 to 10 refer to names of esters.

7. What ester is formed in the reaction of methanol with ethanoic acid?

   A. methyl ethanoate   **B.** ethyl methanoate

8. What ester is formed in the reaction of propanol with methanoic acid?

   A. methyl propanoate   **B.** propyl methanoate

9. What ester is formed in the reaction of ethanoic acid with butanol?

   A. butyl ethanoate   **B.** ethyl butanoate

10. What ester is formed in the reaction of butanoic acid with methanol?

    A. butyl methanoate   **B.** methyl butanoate

In questions 11 to 14, write the name for each of the following esters.

11.

$CH_3-C \begin{smallmatrix} \\ O \\ \\ O-CH_3 \end{smallmatrix}$

13.

$CH_3-CH_2-O-\overset{\overset{\displaystyle O}{\|}}{C}-H$

12.

$CH_3-CH_2-CH_2-O-\overset{\overset{\displaystyle O}{\|}}{C}-CH_3$

14.

$H-C \begin{smallmatrix} \\ O \\ \\ O-CH_3 \end{smallmatrix}$

Questions 15 to 18 refer to structures of esters.

A.

$CH_3-O-\overset{\overset{\displaystyle O}{\|}}{C}-CH_3$

B.

$CH_3-CH_2-C \begin{smallmatrix} \\ O \\ \\ O-CH_3 \end{smallmatrix}$

C.

$CH_3-CH_2-O-\overset{\overset{\displaystyle O}{\|}}{C}-CH_3$

D.

$H-C \begin{smallmatrix} \\ O \\ \\ O-CH_2-CH_3 \end{smallmatrix}$

15.   What is the structure of the ester formed in the reaction between ethanol and methanoic acid?

16.   What is the structure of the ester formed in the reaction between propanoic acid and methanol?

17.   What is the structure of ethyl ethanoate?

18.   What is the structure of methyl ethanoate?

Test 14

In questions 1 to 7 decide whether each of the pairs of compounds are

    A.   isomers   **B.**   **NOT** isomers.

1.

$$Br-\underset{\underset{H}{|}}{\overset{\overset{H}{|}}{C}}-\underset{\underset{H}{|}}{\overset{\overset{H}{|}}{C}}-Br \qquad \text{and} \qquad H-\underset{\underset{Br}{|}}{\overset{\overset{H}{|}}{C}}-\underset{\underset{H}{|}}{\overset{\overset{Br}{|}}{C}}-H$$

2.

$$Br-\underset{\underset{H}{|}}{\overset{\overset{H}{|}}{C}}-\underset{\underset{H}{|}}{\overset{\overset{H}{|}}{C}}-Br \qquad \text{and} \qquad H-\underset{\underset{Br}{|}}{\overset{\overset{Br}{|}}{C}}-\underset{\underset{H}{|}}{\overset{\overset{H}{|}}{C}}-H$$

3.

$$H-\underset{\underset{H}{|}}{\overset{\overset{Br}{|}}{C}}-\underset{\underset{H}{|}}{\overset{\overset{Br}{|}}{C}}-H \qquad \text{and} \qquad H-\underset{\underset{H}{|}}{\overset{\overset{Br}{|}}{C}}-\underset{\underset{Br}{|}}{\overset{\overset{H}{|}}{C}}-H$$

4. $CH_3-CH_2-CH_2-OH$ and $CH_3-\underset{\underset{OH}{|}}{\overset{\overset{H}{|}}{C}}-CH_3$

5. $CH_3-C\overset{\displaystyle O}{\underset{\displaystyle O-CH_3}{<}}$ and $CH_3-CH_2-C\overset{\displaystyle O}{\underset{\displaystyle OH}{<}}$

6. $CH_3-CH_2-CH_2-OH$ and $CH_3-CH_2-C\overset{\displaystyle O}{\underset{\displaystyle OH}{<}}$

7. 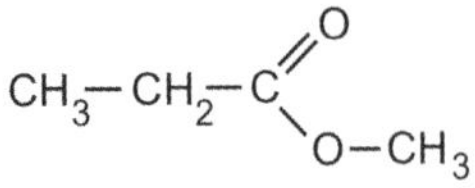 CH_3-CH_2-C (with $=O$ and $O-CH_3$)   and   (structure with $O=$, $C-CH_2-CH_3$, CH_3-O)

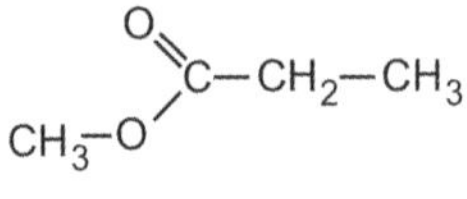

8.   Which compound is an isomer of propanoic acid?

A. 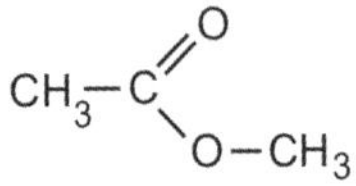 CH_3-C (with $=O$ and $O-CH_3$)

B. 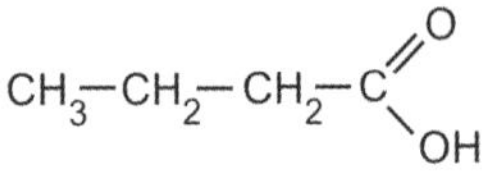 $CH_3-CH_2-CH_2-C$ (with $=O$ and OH)

C. $CH_3-CH_2-CH_2-OH$

D. 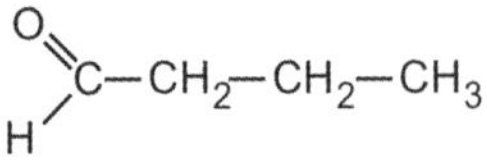   (structure with $O=$, $C-CH_2-CH_2-CH_3$, H)

In questions 9 to 14, decide whether each of the following compounds

A.   has an isomeric form

B.   does **NOT** have an isomeric form.

9. 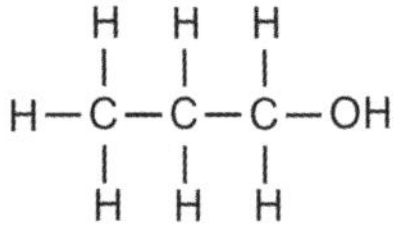
```
      H  H  H
      |  |  |
  H─C─C─C─OH
      |  |  |
      H  H  H
```

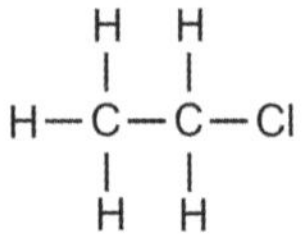

12. 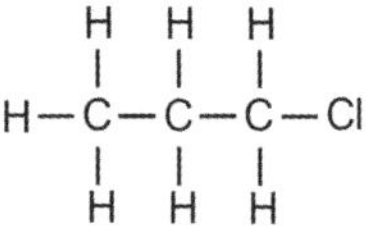
```
      H  H  H
      |  |  |
  H─C─C─C─Cl
      |  |  |
      H  H  H
```

10.
```
  H         H
   \       /
    C=C
   /       \
  H         Cl
```

13. 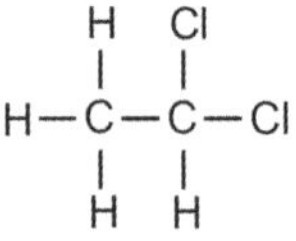
```
      H  Cl
      |  |
  H─C─C─Cl
      |  |
      H  H
```

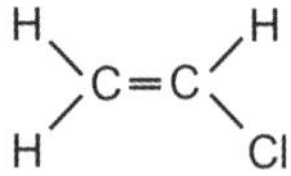

11.
```
      H  H
      |  |
  H─C─C─Cl
      |  |
      H  H
```

14.   methanol

Test 15   Energy from fuels

Calculate the heat energy released by the burning of each the following fuels.

1. The temperature of 100 cm^3 of water is increased by 10 $^{\circ}$C.

2. The temperature of 50 cm^3 of water is increased by 17 $^{\circ}$C.

3. The temperature of 250 cm^3 of water is increased by 6.4 $^{\circ}$C.

4. The temperature of 200 cm^3 of water is increased by 7.1 $^{\circ}$C.

5. The temperature of 100 cm^3 of water is increased from 18 $^{\circ}$C to 39.1 $^{\circ}$C

6. The temperature of 200 cm^3 of water is increased from 15.7 $^{\circ}$C to 23.1 $^{\circ}$C

7. The temperature of 50 cm^3 of water is increased from 16.3 $^{\circ}$C to 23.7 $^{\circ}$C

8. The temperature of 500 cm^3 of water is increased from 17.1 $^{\circ}$C to 27.6 $^{\circ}$C

Test 16   Calculations based on equations

1. $CaCO_3$ ➔ CaO + CO_2

   What mass of carbon dioxide is produced by the decomposition of 10 g calcium carbonate?

2. C_2H_4 + $3O_2$ ➔ $2CO_2$ + $2H_2O$

   What mass of water vapour is produced on burning 7 g of ethene (C_2H_4)?

3. CuO + CO ➔ Cu + CO_2

   What mass of copper oxide must be reduced to give 127 g of copper?

4. $2H_2$ + O_2 ➔ $2H_2O$

   What mass of water vapour is produced on burning 1 g of hydrogen?

5. $2CO$ + O_2 ➔ $2CO_2$

   What mass of carbon monoxide must be burned to give 4.4 g of carbon dioxide?

6. What mass of carbon dioxide is produced on burning 8 g of methane (CH_4)?

7. What mass of hydrogen is required to completely reduce 7.95 g of copper (II) oxide to copper?

8. What mass of hydrogen is obtained when 4.9 g magnesium reacts with excess dilute hydrochloric acid?

9. What mass of sulphur must burn to give 8 g of sulphur dioxide?

10. What mass of propane (C_3H_8) is obtained when 7 g of propene (C_3H_6) reacts with hydrogen?

Test 17   Mixed questions (iii)

Questions 1 and 2 refer to statements which can be applied to hydrocarbons.

    A.   It is saturated.

    B.   It rapidly decolourises bromine water.

    C.   It contains three carbon atoms per molecule.

    D.   It contains a double bond between carbon atoms.

1.   Which statement can be applied to **both** ethane and propane.

2.   Which **two** statements can be applied to propene but **not** to propane.

Questions 3 to 8 refer to the following hydrocarbons.

    A. $CH_3-CH-CH_2-CH_3$ **B.** $CH_3-CH=CH-CH_3$
                       CH_3

    C. $CH_3-CH-CH_3$ **D.** CH_2
                CH_3 CH_2-CH_2

3.   Which **two** hydrocarbons are **not** in the same homologous series as the hydrocarbon with molecular formula C_8H_{18}?

4.   Which hydrocarbon reacts with hydrogen to produce butane?

5.   Which hydrocarbon is an isomer of pentane?

6.   Which hydrocarbon is an isomer of propene?

7.   Which hydrocarbon has the formula C_nH_{2n} but does not react with bromine solution?

8.   Which hydrocarbon has a relative formula mass of 58?

Questions 9 and 10 refer to statements which can be applied to hydrocarbons.

> **A.** It has isomers.
>
> **B.** It has the general formula C_nH_{2n}.
>
> **C.** It takes part in addition reactions.
>
> **D.** It contains only single carbon to carbon bonds.
>
> **E.** It does **NOT** react immediately with bromine water.

9. Which **two** statements can be applied to **both** butene and cyclopropane?

10. Which statement can be applied to butane but **not** to propane?

Questions 11 to 14 refer to the flash points of the hydrocarbons that are shown in the table.

The flash point is the lowest temperature at which the hydrocarbon can vapourise to form a mixture with air that will ignite.

Hydrocarbon	Formula	Flash point / $^\circ$C	Boiling point / $^\circ$C
Hexene	C_6H_{12}	-9	63
Hexane	C_6H_{14}	-23	69
Cyclohexane	C_6H_{12}	-21	81
Heptane	C_7H_{16}	-4	98
Octane	C_8H_{18}	13	126

By referring to the data, decide whether each of the following statements is

> **A.** TRUE   **B.** FALSE.

11. Hexane has a higher flash point than cyclohexane.

12. Octane will **not** flash at $0\ ^\circ$C.

13. The flash points of hydrocarbons increase as the boiling points increase.

14. In a homologous series the flash point increases as the number of carbon atoms increases.

Test 1   The reactivity series

Questions 1 to 4 refer to reactions of the following metals.

A.	gold	**B.**	sodium
C.	magnesium	**D.**	copper

1. Which metal combines with the oxygen of the air and reacts vigorously with water?

2. Which metal reacts with the oxygen of the air when heated but does **not** react with water?

3. Which metal does **not** react with the oxygen of the air and does **not** react with water?

4. Which metal reacts vigorously with the oxygen of the air when heated and reacts slowly with water?

In questions 5 to 10, decide whether each of the following metals

    A.   reacts with dilute acid

    B.   does **NOT** react with dilute acid.

5.	copper	8.	zinc
6.	magnesium	9.	gold
7.	iron	10.	silver

In questions 11 to 16, decide whether each of the following metals is

    A.   found uncombined in the Earth's crust

    B.   **always** found as ores.

11.   silver   14.   sodium

12.   iron   15.   gold

13.   copper   16.   aluminium

Questions 17 to 19 refer to the metals listed below.

    A.   calcium   **B.**   lithium

    C.   gold   **D.**   zinc

17.   Which metal must be stored under oil?

18.   Which metal reacts with water, allowing the gas given off to be safely collected?

19.   Which metal does **not** react with water but reacts with dilute acid?

20.   When two metals were added to (i) cold water and (ii) dilute acid, no difference in activity was observed.

    The metals could have been

    A.   zinc and calcium   **B.**   silver and copper

    C.   lead and magnesium   **D.**   iron and gold.

21. The reaction in the apparatus shown below is used to provide the gas to inflate the balloon.

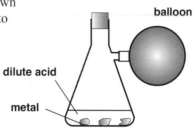

Which of the following metals is the most suitable to use?

    A. copper   **B.** sodium   **C.** magnesium   **D.** silver

Questions 22 to 28 refer to the dates of discovery of metals.

Decide whether each of the following metals was discovered

    A. in the nineteenth century (in the 1800s)

    B. before the nineteenth century (in the 1900s).

22. aluminium

23. gold

24. copper

25. tin

26. calcium

27. sodium

28. iron

Test 2 — Stability of metal oxides

Questions 1 to 4 refer to the heating of metal oxides.

Decide whether each of the following metal oxides

    A. breaks up to give the metal   **B.** does **NOT** break up.

1. sodium oxide   3. copper oxide

2. silver oxide   4. mercury oxide

Questions 5 to 10 refer to the heating of metal oxides with carbon.

Decide whether each of the following metal oxides

    A. breaks up to give the metal   **B.** does **NOT** break up.

5. calcium oxide   8. copper oxide

6. magnesium oxide   9. sodium oxide

7. lead oxide   10. iron oxide

11. Which metal is obtained from its ore by reactions which occur in the Blast Furnace?

    A. copper   **B.** iron   **C.** tin   **D.** zinc

In questions 12 to 15, decide whether each of the following metals

    A. is only obtained from its ore by electrolysis

    B. can be obtained from its ore by a method other than electrolysis.

12. aluminium   14. potassium

13. iron   15. copper

Test 3   Displacement

The questions in this test refer to the addition of metals to ionic solutions.

In each case decide whether a reaction

     A.   takes place

     B.   does **NOT** take place.

(You may wish to use the Data Booklet.)

1. copper added to silver nitrate solution

2. magnesium added to sodium sulphate solution

3. iron added to dilute hydrochloric acid

4. zinc added to copper(II) sulphate solution

5. silver added to potassium chloride solution

6. copper added to dilute sulphuric acid

7. tin added to magnesium nitrate solution

8. silver added to dilute hydrochloric acid

9. iron added to copper(II) nitrate solution

10. magnesium added to dilute sulphuric acid

Test 4   Reactions of metals

1.   An unknown metal was found to be more reactive than sodium.

       Which of the following predictions about the metal is likely to be
       correct?

       A.   It will react readily with the oxygen of the air.

       B.   It should be stored under water.

       C.   Its compounds will be unstable.

       D.   It will be obtained from its oxide by heating with carbon.

2.   Sodium is a very reactive metal.

       Which of the following would be expected to produce sodium?

       A.   passing electricity through molten sodium chloride

       B.   heating sodium oxide in air

       C.   heating sodium oxide with carbon

3.   An unknown metal was found uncombined in the Earth's crust.

       Which of the following predictions about the metal is likely to be
       correct?

       A.   It will be stored under oil.

       B.   Its compounds will be stable.

       C.   It will react with dilute acid.

       D.   Its oxide will decompose on heating.

4. The following facts are known about four metals, **P, Q , R**, and **S**.

(i) **R** displaces **P** and **S** from solutions of their ions;
(ii) **Q** reacts with water, **R** does not;
(iii) only the oxide of metal **S** can be decomposed to give metal on heating.

The order of reactivity (most reactive first) is

A. **R, Q, S, P**   B. **Q, S, P, R**

C. **P, S, Q, R**   D. **Q, R, P, S.**

5. A metallic element reacts with dilute hydrochloric acid releasing hydrogen.
The oxide of the metal can be decomposed by heating with carbon.

From this information alone, the position of the metal in the reactivity series could be between

A. silver and copper   B. zinc and tin

B. magnesium and sodium   D. calcium and aluminium.

6. The following information relates to four metals, **W, X, Y,**and **Z**.

(i) **W** displaces **X** from a solution of its compound;
(ii) only **Z** is stored under oil;
(iii) only the oxide of metal **Y** releases oxygen on heating.

The order of reactivity (most reactive first) is

A. **Y, W, X, Z**   B. **Z, W, X, Y**

C. **Z, X, W, Y**   D. **Y, X, W, Z.**

Test 5   Oxidation and reduction

Decide whether each of the following reactions involve

    A. oxidation   **B.**   reduction.

(You may wish to use the Data Booklet.)

1. Zn^{2+} (aq)   +   2e⁻   ➔   Zn (s)

2.   Ag (s)   ➔ Ag^+ (aq)   +   e⁻

3. Br_2 (l)   +   2e⁻   ➔   2Br- (aq)

4. Sn^{2+} (aq) +   2e⁻   ➔   Sn (s)

5.   2Cl⁻ (aq)   ➔ Cl_2 (g)

6. Mg^{2+} (aq)   ➔   Mg (s)

7.   Fe (s)   ➔ Fe^{2+} (aq)

8. SO_3^{2-} (aq)   ➔ SO_4^{2-} (aq)

9.   nickel(III)   ➔   nickel(II)

10.   cobalt(II)   ➔   cobalt (III)

11.   copper atoms   ➔   copper ions

12.   iodine molecules   ➔   iodide ions.

Test 6

Decide whether each of the following is

    A.   a redox reaction   **B.**   **NOT** a redox reaction.

1. $Zn\,(s)$ + $2H^+\,(aq)$ ➔ $Zn^{2+}\,(aq)$ + $H_2\,(g)$

2. $OH^-\,(aq)$ + $H^+\,(aq)$ ➔ $H_2O\,(l)$

3. $Mg\,(s)$ + $Cu^{2+}\,(aq)$ ➔ $Mg^{2+}\,(aq)$ + $Cu\,(s)$

4. $Ag^+\,(aq)$ + $Cl^-\,(aq)$ ➔ $AgCl\,(s)$

5. $Cl_2\,(g)$ + $2I^-\,(aq)$ ➔ $2Cl^-\,(aq)$ + $I_2\,(aq)$

6. $NH_4^+\,(aq)$ + $OH^-\,(aq)$ ➔ $NH_3\,(g)$ + $H_2O\,(l)$

7. $SnCl_2\,(aq)$ + $HgCl_2\,(aq)$ ➔ $Hg\,(l)$ + $SnCl_4\,(aq)$

8. $C_2H_4\,(g)$ + $Br_2\,(g)$ ➔ $C_2H_4Br_2\,(l)$

9. $2FeO\,(s)$ + $C\,(s)$ ➔ $2Fe\,(s)$ + $CO_2\,(g)$

10. $2Mg\,(s)$ + $O_2\,(g)$ ➔ $2\,MgO\,(s)$

11. $Na_2SO_4\,(aq)$ + $BaCl_2\,(aq)$ ➔ $2NaCl\,(aq)$ + $BaSO_4\,(s)$

12. $CuO\,(s)$ + $2HNO_3\,(aq)$ ➔ $Cu(NO_3)_2\,(aq)$ + $H_2O\,(l)$

13. $F_2\,(g)$ + $2NaBr\,(aq)$ ➔ $Br_2\,(aq)$ + $2NaF\,(aq)$

14. $CaCO_3\,(s)$ ➔ $CaO\,(s)$ + $CO_2\,(g)$

15. $2Na_2S_2O_3\,(aq)$ + $I_2\,(aq)$ ➔ $2NaI\,(aq)$ + $Na_2S_4O_6\,(aq)$

16. $2Na\,(s)$ + $2H_2O\,(l)$ ➔ $2NaOH\,(aq)$ + $H_2\,(g)$

Test 7   Making electricity

Questions 1 to 10 refer to the direction of
electron flow in the apparatus shown.

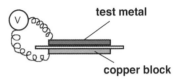

Which is the direction of electron flow when each of the following pairs of test
metals are attached?

1.   **A.**   magnesium to copper.   **B.**   copper to magnesium

2.   **A.**   magnesium to iron   **B.**   iron to magnesium

3.   **A.**   magnesium to silver   **B.**   silver to magnesium

4.   **A.**   magnesium to sodium   **B.**   sodium to magnesium

5.   **A.**   iron to copper   **B.**   copper to iron

6.   **A.**   iron to silver   **B.**   silver to iron

7.   **A.**   iron to sodium   **B.**   sodium to iron

8.   **A.**   silver to copper   **B.**   copper to silver

9.   **A.**   silver to sodium   **B.**   sodium to silver

10.   **A.**   tin to copper   **B.**   copper to tin

Question 11 and 12 refer to the apparatus shown.

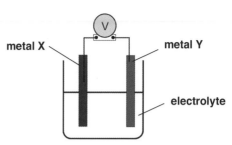

11. Which of the following pairs of metals would give the largest reading on the voltmeter?

   A. iron / zinc   B. silver / magnesium

   C. zinc / copper   D. lead / copper

12. If the voltmeter was replaced by an ammeter which pair of metals would give an electron flow from metal **X** to metal **Y**.

	X	**Y**
A.	zinc	copper
B.	zinc	magnesium
C.	iron	zinc
D.	lead	iron

13. In the apparatus shown below the bulb will become brighter if the copper is replaced by

   A. magnesium

   B. lead

   C. zinc

   D. gold.

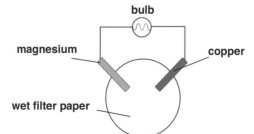

Questions 14 to 17 refer to the following results, which were obtained using the apparatus shown.

Test metal	Voltmeter reading / V
Magnesium	1.6
Iron	0.5
Silver	-0.4
Tin	0.4
Sodium	2.4

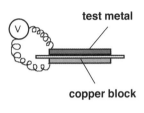

test metal

copper block

14. Which of the metals used in the experiment is best at supplying electrons?

    A. silver   **B.** iron   **C.** sodium   **D.** magnesium

15. Which of the metals used in the experiment is poorest at supplying electrons?

    A. copper   **B.** sodium   **C.** silver   **D.** magnesium

16. If the copper block was replaced by a different test metal, which of the following pairs of metals would give the largest reading on the voltmeter?

    A. silver and tin   **B.** magnesium and tin

    C. silver and sodium   **D.** magnesium and sodium

17. If the copper block was replaced by a block of tin, which metal could be used as the test metal to give a voltmeter reading of approximately 1.2 V?

    A. magnesium   **B.** iron   **C.** sodium   **D.** silver

Questions 18 and 19 refer to the apparatus shown.

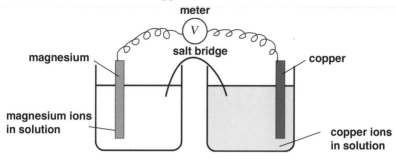

18. Electrons flow from

    A. magnesium to copper through the meter

    B. copper to magnesium through the meter

    C. magnesium to copper through the ion bridge

    D. copper to magnesium through the ion bridge.

19. Which of the following metals/metal ions can replace the magnesium/magnesium ions and produce a flow of electrons in the opposite direction?

    A. zinc   B. gold   C. iron   D. lead

In questions 20 to 25, decide whether aqueous solutions of each of the following is

    A. suitable for use in a salt bridge

    B. **NOT** suitable for use in a salt bridge.

20. sodium chloride   23. ammonium sulphate

21. sucrose ($C_{12}H_{22}O_{11}$)   24. glucose ($C_6H_{12}O_6$)

22. ethanol (C_2H_5OH)   25. potassium nitrate

Test 8   Using electricity

Questions 1 to 6 refer to what happens at the negative electrode during the electrolysis of lead iodide melt.

Decide whether each of the following statements is

    A. TRUE   **B.**   FALSE.

1. lead metal appears

2. iodide ions are reduced

3. lead atoms are reduced

4. lead ions are reduced

5. lead ions are oxidised

6. iodide ions are oxidised

Questions 7 to 12 refer to what happens at the positive electrode during the electrolysis of copper chloride solution.

Decide whether each of the following statements is

    A. TRUE   **B.**   FALSE.

7. copper metal is formed

8. chlorine is formed

9. copper ions are reduced

10. chloride ions are reduced

11. chloride ions are oxidised

12. chlorine atoms are oxidised

Test 9   Corrosion (i)

1. The corrosion of which metal is called rusting?

    A. copper   **B.** silver

    C. tin   **D.** iron

2. Which of the following solutions is used to show the extent of the rusting process?

    A. Universal indicator   **B.** lime water

    C. ferroxyl indicator   **D.** bromine solution

Questions 3 to 7 refer to experiments which are set up to investigate the speed of rusting.

In each of the following cases, decide in which experiment the iron nail will rust faster.

3. **A.**  tap water   **B.** 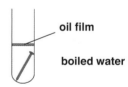 oil film / boiled water

4. **A.** 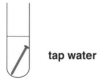 tap water   **B.**  drying agent

5. **A.**  tap water   **B.**  sea water

6. **A.**

tap water

B.

tap water in 'acid rain' area

7. **A.**

battery
+ve -ve

iron plate

B.

battery
-ve +ve

iron plate

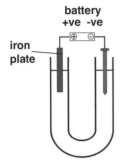

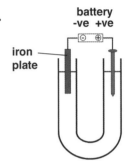

Questions 8 to 13 refer to the attaching of different metals to an iron nail.

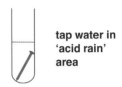

metal

Decide whether each of the following metals

    A.   protects the iron nail from corrosion

    B.   does **NOT** protect the iron nail from corrosion.

8.   tin

9.   magnesium

10. silver

11. copper

12. zinc

13. lead

Questions 14 to 19 refer to an iron gate which has been galvanised, i.e. coated with zinc.

The gate has been scratched to expose the iron.

Decide whether each of the following statements is

    A. TRUE   **B.** FALSE.

14.   The zinc increases the rate of corrosion of iron.

15.   The zinc atoms lose electrons.

16.   The zinc attracts electrons from the iron.

17.   The zinc does **not** corrode.

18.   The zinc corrodes slower than the iron.

19.   The zinc is sacrificed to protect the iron.

Questions 20 to 24 refer to a gas pipeline made from iron which is protected by attaching scrap magnesium.

Decide whether each of the following statements is

    A. TRUE   **B.** FALSE.

20.   The magnesium atoms lose electrons.

21.   The magnesium does **not** corrode.

22.   The iron corrodes faster than the magnesium.

23.   The magnesium provides sacrificial protection.

24.   Electrons flow from the iron to the magnesium.

Questions 25 to 27 refer to methods for protecting iron from corrosion.

A. electroplating   **B.** galvanising   **C.** sacrificial protection

25.   What name is given to the process in which iron is dipped into molten zinc to give it a protective layer?

26.   What name is given to the process in which scrap magnesium is used to protect an iron structure?

27.   What name is given to the process in which electrolysis is used to coat iron with another metal?

28.   Corrosion of iron can be prevented by putting a barrier of another metal between the iron and the atmosphere.

A coating of which metal will lead to sacrificial protection if the barrier is broken?

A. copper   **B.** silver   **C.** tin   **D.** zinc

29.   Small metal plates can be fixed to the iron chassis of a car to reduce corrosion.

These plates could be made of

A. tin   **B.** calcium   **C.** magnesium   **D.** copper.

30.   In which of the following situations is sacrificial corrosion useful?

A. iron cans plated with tin

B. iron plates riveted with copper rivets

C. steel ships fitted with zinc below the water line

D. lead connected to iron pipes

Questions 31 to 34 refer to the riveting of metal plates.

Riveted metal plates can loosen due to corrosion of the metal rivets.

In each of the following cases, decide whether

A. the plates corrode before the rivets

B. the rivets corrode before the plates.

31. copper plates and iron rivets   33. silver plates with copper rivets

32. zinc plates and aluminium rivets   34. iron plates and copper rivets

35. When a cell is set up with iron and an unknown metal **X**, the electron flow in the external circuit is from iron to **X**.

Which of the following statements is a correct deduction from this observation?

A. It will be possible to use metal **X** for the sacrificial protection of iron.

B. Corrosion of metal **X** in air is likely to be rapid.

C. An iron container coated with metal **X** will not corrode even when the coating is broken.

D. It will be unwise to use rivets made of metal **X** in an iron structure.

36. Galvanising and tin-plating are two methods of protecting iron from corrosion. They work equally well until the protective layer is broken.

The galvanised iron then lasts longer because

A. galvanising gives thicker plating than tin plating

B. zinc is higher in the reactivity series than iron

C. tin is higher in the reactivity series than zinc

D. galvanising increases the thickness of the oxide coat on the iron.

Test 10   Corrosion (ii)

1. During corrosion, the reaction involving the metal is an example of

     A.   oxidation   **B.**   reduction.

Questions 2 to 7 refer to the diagram opposite.

Decide whether each of the following substances,
when added to the water,

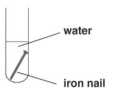

     A.   would be expected to increase the speed of rusting

     B.   would **NOT** be expected to increase the speed of rusting.

2.	carbon dioxide	5.	sucrose
3.	starch	6.	salt
4.	potassium nitrate	7.	calcium carbonate

Questions 8 to 10 refer to cells with an iron nail as one of the electrodes.

The iron nail is immersed in a gel with ferroxyl indicator and an electrolyte.

8. In the cell shown opposite,
   a blue colour will appear at

   A.   the carbon rod

   B.   the iron nail

   C.   **neither** the carbon rod
          nor the iron nail

   D.   **both** the carbon rod
          and the iron nail.

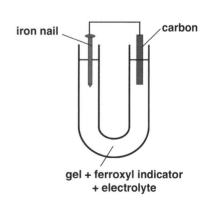

9. In the cell shown opposite, a blue colour will appear at

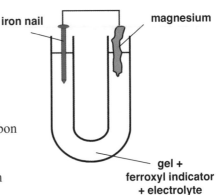

iron nail   magnesium

gel +
ferroxyl indicator
+ electrolyte

A. the magnesium ribbon

B. the iron nail

C. **neither** the magnesium ribbon
    nor the iron nail

D. **both** the magnesium ribbon
    and the iron nail.

10. In the cell shown opposite, a blue colour will appear at

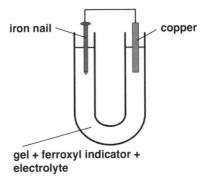

iron nail   copper

gel + ferroxyl indicator +
electrolyte

A. the copper foil

B. the iron nail

C. **neither** the copper foil
    nor the iron nail

D. **both** the copper foil
    and the iron nail.

Questions 11 to 16 refer to the following experiment.

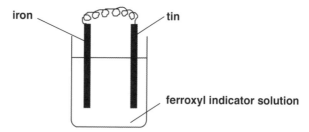

Decide whether each of the following statements is

A.　TRUE　　　　　　　　　　B.　　FALSE.

11.　Tin atoms are oxidised.

12.　Iron ions are reduced.

13.　A blue colour forms around the iron.

14.　The mass of iron decreases.

15.　The electrons flow through the wire from the tin.

16.　A pink colour forms around the tin.

Test 11 ***

Plastics

Decide whether each of the following statements is

    A. TRUE   **B.** FALSE.

1. Plastics are good conductors of heat.

2. Most plastics are biodegradable.

3. Some plastics burn or smoulder to give off toxic fumes.

4. A thermoplastic melts on heating.

5. Plastics are examples of electrical insulators.

6. Plastics are examples of monomers.

7. Polythene is a plastic made from ethene.

8. A thermosetting plastic can be easily reshaped.

9. Styrene is an example of a polymer.

10. Many plastics are made from methane (natural gas).

11. Plastics can be made by polymerisation reactions.

12. Polystyrene is a plastic made from propene.

13. Polystyrene can be used for packaging because it is light.

14. Waste plastics can be recycled to make new products.

15. Butene is a monomer used to make poly(butene).

16. Biopol is a recently developed biodegradable plastic.

17. The main reason for using Kevlar to make bullet-proof vests is that it is very light.

18. Poly(ethenol) is soluble in water.

Test 12   **Addition polymerisation**

Questions 1 to 4 refer to the part of the polymer shown below.

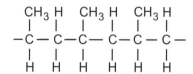

1.   How many repeating units are shown?

      A. 2   **B.** 3   **C.** 6   **D.** 9

2.   What is the repeating unit?

      A.   **B.**

      C.   **D.**

3.   What is the name of the monomer?

      A. ethene   **B.** propane

      C. propene   **D.** butane

4.   What is the name of the polymer?

      A. polythene   **B.** poly(propene)

      C. poly(butene)   **D.** P.V.C.

5. Acrilan is an addition polymer made from acrylonitrile. The structural formula for acrylonitrile is:

```
    H   H
    |   |
    C = C
    |   |
    H   CN
```

Which of the following is part of the structure of Acrilan?

A.
```
    H   H   H   H
    |   |   |   |
  — C — C — C — C —
    |   |   |   |
    H  CN   H  CN
```

B.
```
    H   H       H   H
    |   |       |   |
  — C — C = N — C — C = N —
    |           |
    CH₃         CH₃
```

C.
```
    H   H       H   H
    |   |       |   |
  = C — C — N = C — C — N =
        |           |
        H           H
```

D.
```
   CN   H      CN   H
    |   |       |   |
  — C — C — C — C —
    |   |       |   |
    H  CN   H  CN
```

6. Polyvinyl chloride is a polymer of vinyl chloride, $CH_2 = CHCl$ (chloroethene).

Which of the following is part of the structure of polyvinyl chloride?

A.
```
   Cl  Cl  Cl  Cl
    |   |   |   |
  — C — C — C — C —
    |   |   |   |
    H   H   H   H
```

B.
```
    H  Cl   H  Cl
    |   |   |   |
  — C — C — C — C —
    |   |   |   |
    Cl  H  Cl   H
```

C.
```
    H  Cl   H  Cl
    |   |   |   |
  — C — C — C — C —
    |   |   |   |
    H   H   H   H
```

D.
```
    H  Cl   H  Cl
    |   |   |   |
  — C = C — C = C —
```

7.

$$\begin{array}{ccccccc} & \text{CH}_3 & \text{H} & \text{CH}_3 & \text{H} & \text{CH}_3 & \text{H} \\ & | & | & | & | & | & | \\ -\text{C} & - & \text{C} & - \text{C} & - & \text{C} & - \text{C} & - \text{C} & - \\ & | & | & | & | & | & | \\ & \text{Cl} & \text{H} & \text{Cl} & \text{H} & \text{Cl} & \text{H} \end{array}$$

Which monomer could polymerise to give the above polymer?

A.
$$\begin{array}{ccc} \text{H} & \text{H} & \text{H} \\ | & | & | \\ \text{C} = \text{C} - \text{C} - \text{CH}_3 \\ | & & | \\ \text{H} & & \text{Cl} \end{array}$$

B.
$$\begin{array}{c} \text{H} \\ | \\ \text{CH}_3 - \text{C} = \text{C} - \text{CH}_3 \\ | \\ \text{Cl} \end{array}$$

C.
$$\begin{array}{cc} \text{H} & \text{H} \\ | & | \\ \text{CH}_3 - \text{C} = \text{C} \\ & | \\ & \text{Cl} \end{array}$$

D.
$$\begin{array}{c} \text{H} \\ | \\ \text{CH}_3 - \text{C} = \text{C} \\ | \quad | \\ \text{Cl} \quad \text{H} \end{array}$$

8. Which monomer could polymerise to give the polymer shown?

$$\begin{array}{ccccccc} & \text{CH}_3 & \text{H} & \text{CH}_3 & \text{H} & \text{CH}_3 & \text{H} \\ & | & | & | & | & | & | \\ -\text{C} & - & \text{C} & - \text{C} & - & \text{C} & - \text{C} & - \text{C} & - \\ & | & | & | & | & | & | \\ & \text{CN} & \text{H} & \text{CN} & \text{H} & \text{CN} & \text{H} \end{array}$$

A.
$$\begin{array}{cc} \text{CH}_3 & \text{CH}_3 \\ | & | \\ \text{C} = \text{C} \\ | & | \\ \text{CN} & \text{H} \end{array}$$

B.
$$\begin{array}{cc} \text{H} & \text{CH}_3 \\ | & | \\ \text{C} = \text{C} \\ | & | \\ \text{CN} & \text{CH}_3 \end{array}$$

C.
$$\begin{array}{cc} \text{H} & \text{CH}_3 \\ | & | \\ \text{C} = \text{C} \\ | & | \\ \text{CN} & \text{H} \end{array}$$

D.
$$\begin{array}{cc} \text{CH}_3 & \text{H} \\ | & | \\ \text{C} = \text{C} \\ | & | \\ \text{CN} & \text{H} \end{array}$$

9. Part of a polymer molecule is represented below.

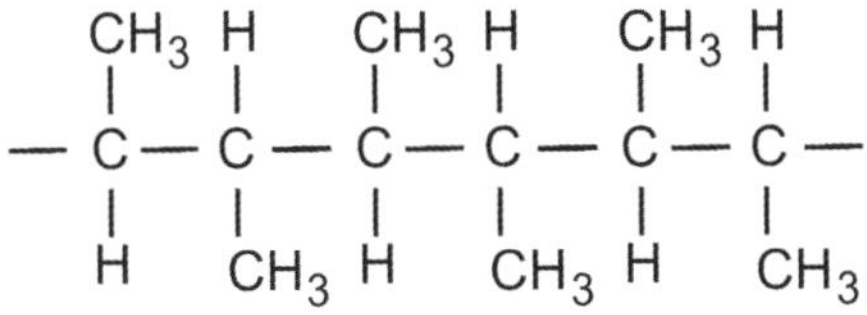

$$
\begin{array}{cccccc}
CH_3 & H & CH_3 & H & CH_3 & H \\
| & | & | & | & | & | \\
-C- & C- & C- & C- & C- & C- \\
| & | & | & | & | & | \\
H & CH_3 & H & CH_3 & H & CH_3
\end{array}
$$

Which monomer could polymerise to give the above polymer?

A. $CH_2 = CH - CH_2 - CH_3$

B. $CH_3 - CH = CH - CH_3$

C. $CH_3 - CH = CH_2$

D. $CH_2 = CH_2$.

10. Part of a polymer molecule is shown.

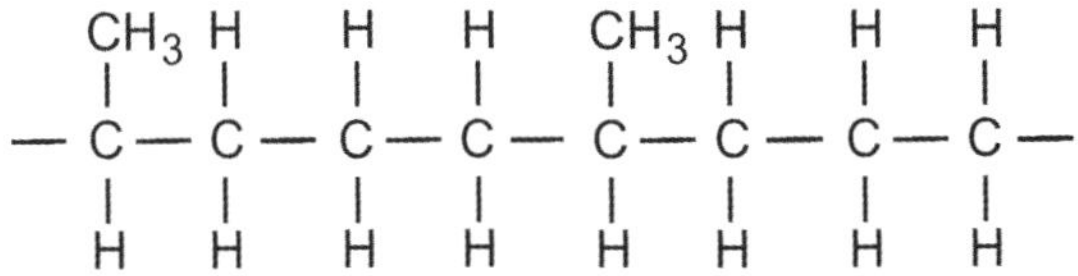

$$
\begin{array}{cccccccc}
CH_3 & H & H & H & CH_3 & H & H & H \\
| & | & | & | & | & | & | & | \\
-C- & C- & C- & C- & C- & C- & C- & C- \\
| & | & | & | & | & | & | & | \\
H & H & H & H & H & H & H & H
\end{array}
$$

The polymer is made from

A. propene monomer only

B. butene monomer only

C. both ethene and propene monomers

D. both ethene and butene monomers.

Test 13 ***   Fertilisers

Decide whether each of the following statements is

A. TRUE   **B.** FALSE.

1. The increasing world population has led to a need for more efficient food production.

2. Fertilisers are substances which can restore the essential elements for plant growth to the soil.

3. A good fertiliser is a substance which is insoluble in water.

4. The healthy growth of plants requires nutrients, including compounds of nitrogen.

5. Phosphorus compounds are useful fertilisers.

6. Animal manure is an example of a synthetic fertiliser.

7. Town sewage can be treated to produce fertiliser.

8. Over-use of synthetic fertilisers can cause environmental problems.

9. Compost can be useful to replace nitrogen compounds in the soil.

10. The eating of plants by animals is a step in the nitrogen cycle.

11. Natural fertilisers are made by industrial processes.

12. Fertilisers are used to replace nitrogen which is lost from the nitrogen cycle.

13. Essential nutrients are taken in through the roots of plants, as compounds dissolved in water.

14. Sodium chloride is a better fertiliser than potassium nitrate.

15. In times of heavy rain, fertilisers can be washed out of the soil.

Test 14

The industrial manufacture
of ammonia

Decide whether each of the following statements is

     A. TRUE   **B.**   FALSE.

1. Ammonia is made in industry from nitrogen and water.

2. The reaction is likely to be carried out at a very low temperature.

3. Ammonia is used to make fertilisers.

4. The reaction is named the Haber Process.

5. An iron catalyst is used in the reaction.

6. Ammonia gas is cooled to remove it from the unchanged reactants.

7. The nitrogen for the reaction is obtained from nitrogen oxides.

8. The gases in the reaction chamber are kept at low pressure.

9. The catalyst is used to prevent the ammonia decomposing.

10. One of the reactants is obtained from methane (natural gas).

11. All the reactants are converted to ammonia.

12. Ammonia is produced from nitrogen and hydrogen.

13. The catalyst speeds up the formation of ammonia.

14. The word equation for the reaction is:

    nitrogen oxide + hydrogen ➜ ammonia + oxygen

15. The unchanged reactants can be recycled.

16. The nitrogen for the reaction is obtained by fractional distilation of liquid air.

Test 15

The industrial manufacture of nitric acid

In questions 1 to 5, decide whether each of the following statements is

    A. TRUE   **B.** FALSE.

1. The oxidation of nitrogen is the first step in the process.

2. In the presence of air, nitrogen dioxide dissolves in water to form nitric acid.

3. The industrial manufacture of nitric acid is called the Ostwald Process.

4. The reaction that takes place on the catalyst is endothermic.

5. Ammonia gas reacts on the catalyst.

6. What are the products of the reaction that takes place on the catalyst?

    A. nitrogen and hydrogen

    B. water and oxides of nitrogen

    C. nitrogen and water

    D. hydrogen and oxides of nitrogen

7. What catalyst is normally used in this process?

    A. iron

    B. vanadium pentoxide

    C. aluminium oxide

    D. platinum

Test 16   Percentage mass

In questions 1 to 10, calculate the percentage (by mass) of each of the elements present in the following compounds.

1. H_2O

2. C_2H_6

3. $CaCl_2$

4.   NaOH

5. K_2CO_3

6. $LiNO_3$

7. C_3H_6O

8. $Al(OH)_3$

9. $FeSO_4$

10. $(NH_4)_3PO_4$

11. Find the most useful fertiliser by calculating which has the highest percentage mass of nitrogen.

   A. $CO(NH_2)_2$ **B.** $(NH_4)_2SO_4$ **C.** NH_4NO_3

12. Calculate the mass of potassium in 1 kg of potassium nitrate, KNO_3 .

Test 17

Types of radiation

The questions in this test refer to types of radiation.

    A.   alpha radiation   **B.**   beta radiation   **C.**   gamma radiation

1.   What name is given to the electrons which are emitted from the nucleus of certain radioactive atoms?

2.   What name is given to the particles consisting of 2 protons and 2 neutrons?

3.   What name is given to the electromagnetic radiations of a very short wavelength?

4.   Which is the most penetrating radiation?

5.   Which is the least penetrating radiation?

6.   Which radiation is attracted by a positive electric field?

7.   Which radiation is attracted by a negative electric field?

8.   Which radiation passes through an electric field without deflection?

9.   What radiation is represented by $_{-1}^{0}e$?

10.   What radiation is represented by $_{2}^{4}He^{2+}$?

11.   Which radiation has no mass associated with it?

12.   Which radiation is a pure form of energy?

Test 18   Changes in the nucleus

1. The stability of the nucleus of an ion depends on the ratio of

    A. mass : charge   **B.** neutrons : protons

    C. neutrons : electrons   **D.** protons : electrons.

Questions 2 to 4 refer to changes in the nucleus.

	Atomic number	Mass number
A.	increased	no change
B.	decreased	decreased
C.	no change	increased
D.	no change	no change
E.	increased	increased

2. Which change is associated with beta emission.

3. Which change is associated with alpha emission.

4. Which change is associated with gamma emission.

In questions 5 to 8, decide whether each of the following nuclear reactions involves

    A. alpha emission   **B.** beta emission.

5. $^{23}_{11}Na$ $\rightarrow$ $^{23}_{12}Mg$ 7. ^{241}Am $\rightarrow$ ^{237}Np

6. $^{238}_{92}U$ $\rightarrow$ $^{234}_{90}Th$ 8. ^{14}C $\rightarrow$ ^{14}N

In questions 9 to 16, decide whether each of the following nuclear reactions involves

    A.   alpha emission

    B.   beta emission

    C.   **neither** alpha **nor** beta emission.

9. $^{81}_{36}Kr$ ➔ $^{81}_{35}Br$

10. $^{210}_{84}Po$ ➔ $^{206}_{82}Pb$

11. $^{207}_{82}Pb$ ➔ $^{208}_{83}Bi$

12. $^{228}_{88}Ra$ ➔ $^{228}_{89}Ac$

13. ^{23}Na ➔ ^{24}Na

14. ^{3}H ➔ ^{3}He

15. ^{222}Rn ➔ ^{218}Po

16. ^{228}Pa ➔ ^{227}Pa

17.   What element is formed when an atom of radium emits a beta particle?

    A.   radon   **B.**   francium

    C.   actinium   **D.**   thorium

18.   Protactinium-231 is formed by beta emission from a radioisotope of thorium.

    What is the mass number of the radioisotope of thorium?

    A.   230   **B.**   231   **C.**   232   **D.**   235.

19. What is formed when radium-224 emits an alpha particle?

A. radon-220 B. radon-222

C. actinium-224 D. thorium-228.

20. A radioactive atom of a Group 4 element emits one beta particle.

The decay product will be an atom of an element in

A. Group 3 B. Group 4

C. Group 5 D. Group 6.

21. An element in Group 4 is formed by alpha emission.

The radioactive isotope which decays to form the element will be in

A. Group 2 B. Group 3

C. Group 5 D. Group 6.

22. Radioactive ^{14}C decays by beta particle emission.

Which statement is true of the new nucleus formed?

A. It has mass number 13. B. It has 6 protons.

C. It has 7 neutrons. D. It is a carbon nucleus.

23. When an atom of ^{239}U emits a beta particle, the product formed also decays, emitting another beta particle.

The atom formed after the second emission is

A. ^{238}Ra B. ^{239}Th C. ^{238}U D. ^{239}Pu.

24. Which series of transformations would produce an atom of the same element as at the start?

   A.   alpha, beta, beta

   B.   beta, alpha, alpha

   C.   beta, gamma

   D.   alpha, beta

25. What particle will be formed when an atom of ^{211}Bi loses an alpha particle and the decay product then loses a beta particle?

   A. ^{210}Au   **B.** ^{209}Hg   **C.** ^{207}Tl   **D.** ^{207}Pb

26. The following represents part of a natural radioactive decay series.

   ^{x}U ^{y}Th   → ^{231}Pa

   Which of the following represent the mass numbers **x** and **y**?

	x	y
A.	239	235
B.	232	231
C.	237	233
D.	235	231

Test 19   Half-life

1.   When some zinc pellets containing radioactive zinc are placed in a solution of zinc chloride, radioactivity soon appears in the solution.

Compared to the pellets, the half-life of the radioactive solution will be

A.   shorter

B.   the same

C.   longer

D.   dependent upon how long the zinc is in contact with the solution.

2.   When some lead pellets containing radioactive lead are placed in a solution of lead nitrate, radioactivity soon appears in the solution.

Compared to the pellets the solution will show

A.   different intensity of radiation and different half-life

B.   the same intensity of radiation but different half-life

C.   different intensity of radiation but the same half-life

D.   the same intensity of radiation and the same half-life.

3   The half-life of bismuth in 1g of bismuth oxide compared to 1g bismuth sulphate will be

A.   greater because the percentage of bismuth is greater

B.   less because of the greater stability of the smaller oxide ion

C.   the same because the half-life is independent of the percentage of bismuth

D.   impossible to predict.

Questions 4 and 5 refer to the different masses of two substances containing ^{224}Ra, an alpha emitter.

  A. 1 g of radium   **B.** 10 g of radium

  C. 1 g of radium chloride   **D.** 10 g of radium chloride

4. In which substance will the intensity of radiation be least?

5. In which substance will the intensity of radiation be greatest?

6. Radioactive uranium is present in rocks in the form of compounds like uranium(IV) oxide.   When the rock is processed, a large amount of the uranium can be recovered as pure metal.

    Compared to the original rock, the half-life of the pure metal will be

    A. shorter

    B. the same

    C. longer

    D. dependent upon the amount that is recovered.

7. Which of the following processes, if any, would alter the half-life of a sample of radioactive calcium?

    A. cooling it to -50 $^{\circ}$C

    B. dissolving it in dilute hydrochloric acid

    C. burning it in air

    D. none of these

8. The half-life of tritium, ^3H, is 12.4 years. In a bottle of old wine, the ^3H level is found to be 1/16 th of that in new wine.

The wine was approximately

 A. 40 years old   **B.** 50 years old

 C. 60 years old   **D.** 100 years old.

9. ^{24}Na is a beta emitter with a half-life of 15 hours.

What percentage of the original isotope would remain after 45 hours?

 A. 12.5   **B.** 25   **C.** 33.3   **D.** 75

10. ^{14}C has a half-life of 5600 years. An analysis of charcoal from a wood fire shows that its ^{14}C content is 25% that of living wood.

How many years have passed since the wood for the fire was cut?

 A. 1400   **B.** 4200   **C.** 11 200   **D.** 16 800

11. After 48 years the level of radioactivity in a sample of an isotope was found to be 1/8 th of the level originally.

What is the half-life of the isotope?

 A. 6 years   **B.** 12 years   **C.** 16 years   **D.** 24 years

12. ^{215}Tl is a beta emitter with a half-life of 4.2 minutes.

What percentage of the original isotope would remain after 8.4 minutes?

 A. 12.5   **B.** 25   **C.** 50   **D.** 75

Test 20 Qualitative and quantitative analysis

Decide whether each of the following techniques is an example of

  A. qualitative analysis   **B.** quantitative analysis.

1. finding the pH of a solution

2. a flame test for potassium

3. testing for nitrate ions in river water

4. finding the concentration of chloride ions in a swimming pool

5. using litmus paper to find out whether or not a solution is alkaline

6. determining the mass of cerium in cigarette lighter flints

7. detecting chloride ions in a water sample

8. finding the percentage purity of a metal salt

9. finding the volume of ozone in a litre of air

10. monitoring the presence of lead in water pipes

11. using bromine water to identify the presence of an alkene

12. carrying out a titration to find the concentration of an acid.

13. using a breathalyser to measure the amount of alcohol that has been consumed

Test 21   Mixed questions (iv)

Questions 1 and 2 refer to statements which can be applied to metals.

    A.   It reacts with dilute acid.

    B.   It reacts quickly with cold water.

    C.   It reacts when heated with oxygen.

    D.   It reacts with zinc sulphate solution.

    E.   It reacts with silver nitrate solution.

    F.   It reacts with sodium chloride solution.

1.   Which **two** statements can be applied to **both** aluminium and copper?

2.   Which statement can be applied to magnesium but **not** to lead?

Questions 3 and 4 refer to the following ion-electron equations.

    A. $Fe(s) \rightarrow Fe^{2+}(aq) + 2e^-$

    B. $Fe^{2+}(aq) + 2e^- \rightarrow Fe(s)$

    C. $Fe^{2+}(aq) \rightarrow Fe^{3+}(aq) + e^-$

    D. $Fe^{3+}(aq) + e^- \rightarrow Fe^{2+}(aq)$

    E. $Cu(s) \rightarrow Cu^{2+}(aq) + 2e^-$

    F. $Cu^{2+}(aq) + 2e^- \rightarrow Cu(s)$

3.   Which equation shows iron(II) ions being oxidised?

4.   Which **two** equations show the reactions which occur when an iron nail is placed in copper(II) sulphate solution?

Questions 5 and 6 refer to statements which can be applied to reactions of metals.

    A.   It displaces lead from a solution of lead nitrate.

    B.   It reacts with cold water.

    C.   It can be obtained by heating its oxide with carbon.

    D.   It reacts with dilute hydrochloric acid.

    E.   It is displaced from a solution of its chloride by zinc.

  5.   Which **two** statements can be applied to **both** magnesium and tin?

  6.   Which **two** statements can be applied to iron but **not** copper?

Questions 7 to 11 refer to experiments involving magnesium, zinc, copper, tin, silver and unknown metal **X**.

From all of their observations, a group of students produced the following order of reactivity.

          silver, **X**, copper, tin, zinc, magnesium

                     Increasing reactivity

Decide whether each of the following observations

    A.   can be used to show that **X** has been wrongly placed

    B.   can **NOT** be used to show that **X** has been wrongly placed.

  7.   Compounds of **X** were more readily reduced than compounds of zinc.

  8.   **X** oxide was more stable to heat than silver oxide.

  9.   **X** was more readily oxidised than copper.

 10.   Magnesium displaced **X** from a solution of **X** nitrate.

 11.   **X** reacted more vigorously with dilute acid than did tin.

Questions 12 to 16 refer to the voltages between pairs of metals.

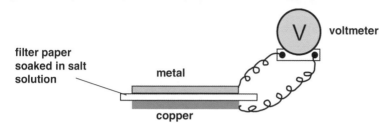

Metal	Voltage / V	Direction of electron flow
P	0.6	metal ➜ copper
Q	0.2	copper ➜ metal
R	0.9	metal ➜ copper
S	0.1	copper ➜ metal

Decide whether each of the following statements is

    A. TRUE   **B.** FALSE.

12. Metal **P** is the least reactive metal.

13. Metal **R** is found uncombined in the Earth's crust.

14. Metals **Q** and **S** are the easiest to obtain from their compounds.

15. Metal **R** displaces all the other metals from solutions of their salts.

16. Metals **P** and **R** give a higher voltage than any other pair when connected in a cell.

Chemical tests ***

Questions 1 and 2 refer to colourless gases.

A.	hydrogen	**B.**	oxygen
C.	nitrogen	**D.**	carbon dioxide

1. Which gas relights a glowing splint?

2. Which gas burns with a 'pop'?

Questions 3 to 9 refer to solutions which are used in the laboratory for chemical tests.

A.	Benedict's solution	**B.**	bromine solution
C.	ferroxyl indicator	**D.**	iodine solution
E.	Universal indicator	**F.**	lime water

Which solution is used to test for each of the following?

3. an acid

4. carbon dioxide

5. the Fe^{2+} ions produced in rusting

6. an alkali

7. an unsaturated hydrocarbon

8. glucose

9. starch

Question 10 to 15 refer to tests for gases.

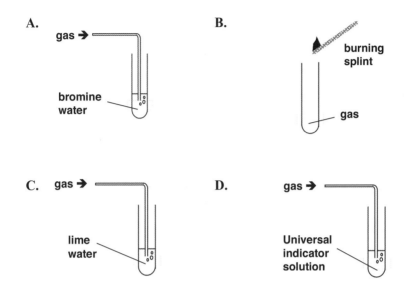

A. gas → bromine water

B. burning splint — gas

C. gas → lime water

D. gas → Universal indicator solution

Which test can be used to quickly distinguish each of the following gases from nitrogen?

(Note that for some questions, more than one response may be correct.)

10.   oxygen

11.   carbon dioxide

12.   methane

13.   sulphur dioxide

14.   hydrogen

15.   butane

Types of reactions

The questions in this test refer to types of reaction.

    A. displacement   **B.** neutralisation

    C. precipitation   **D.** redox

(Note that for some questions, more than one response may be correct.)

Which type(s) of reaction can be applied to each of the following?

1.   Zinc reacts with dilute hydrochloric acid.

2.   Solid barium sulphate is produced by mixing barium chloride solution with sodium sulphate solution.

3.   Sodium hydroxide reacts with dilute hydrochloric acid.

4.   Magnesium reacts with silver nitrate solution.

5.   Dilute nitric acid reacts with sodium carbonate.

6.   Magnesium combines with oxygen to form magnesium oxide.

7. $AgNO_3\,(aq) \quad + \quad NaCl\,(aq) \quad \rightarrow \quad AgCl(s) \quad + \quad NaNO_3\,(aq)$

8. $Fe_2O_3\,(s) \quad + \quad 3CO(g) \quad \rightarrow \quad 2Fe(s) \quad + \quad 3CO_2\,(g)$

9. $Mg\,(s) \quad + \quad H_2SO_4\,(aq) \quad \rightarrow \quad MgSO_4\,(aq) \quad + \quad H_2\,(g)$

10. $KOH\,(aq) \quad + \quad HNO_3\,(aq) \quad \rightarrow \quad KNO_3\,(aq) \quad + \quad H_2O\,(l)$

11. $Zn\,(s) \quad + \quad CuSO_4\,(aq) \quad \rightarrow \quad Cu\,(s) \quad + \quad ZnSO_4\,(aq)$

12. $CuO\,(s) \quad + \quad H_2SO_4\,(aq) \quad \rightarrow \quad CuSO_4\,(aq) \quad + \quad H_2O\,(l)$

13. $CaCO_3\,(s) \quad + \quad 2HNO_3\,(aq) \quad \rightarrow \quad Ca(NO_3)_2\,(aq) \quad + \quad CO_2\,(s) \quad + \quad H_2O\,(l)$

14. $OH^-\,(aq) \quad + \quad H^+\,(aq) \quad \rightarrow \quad H_2O\,(l)$

15. $Ca^{2+}\,(aq) \quad + \quad 2F^-\,(aq) \quad \rightarrow \quad CaF_2\,(s)$

16. $2H^+\,(aq) \quad + \quad CO_3^{2-}\,(aq) \quad \rightarrow \quad H_2O\,(l) \quad + \quad CO_2\,(g)$

17. $Mg\,(s) \quad + \quad 2Ag^+\,(aq) \quad \rightarrow \quad Mg^{2+}\,(aq) \quad + \quad 2Ag\,(s)$

Using the data booklet

1. Which element was the first to be discovered?

   A. fluorine   **B.** lithium   **C.** magnesium **D.** phosphorus

2. Which element has the highest density?

   A. copper   **B.** iron   **C.** silver   **D.** zinc

3. Which element has the highest melting point?

   A. chlorine   **B.** fluorine   **C.** nitrogen   **D.** oxygen

4. Which element has a boiling point of 280 $^\circ$C?

   A. aluminium **B.** calcium   **C.** phosphorus **D.** sodium

5. Which compound has a melting point of 714 $^\circ$C?

   A. barium chloride   **B.** lithium bromide

   C. magnesium chloride   **D.** potassium iodide

6. Which liquid has a boiling point of 69 $^\circ$C?

   A. pentane   **B.** hexane   **C.** heptane   **D.** octane

7. Which element has a red flame colour?

   A. barium   **B.** copper   **C.** lithium   **D.** sodium

8. A space probe sent to study the surface of the planet Mars would need to be made of a metal which would not melt at 510 $^\circ$C.

   Which metal could be used in this probe?

   A. magnesium   **B.** lead   **C.** tin   **D.** zinc

In questions 9 to 14, decide whether each of the following compounds is

A. soluble in water **B.** insoluble in water.

9. calcium carbonate

10. potassium chloride

11. iron(III) nitrate

12. barium sulphate

13. lead(II) iodide

14. sodium bromide

In questions 15 to 24, decide whether each of the following substances, at the stated temperature, is

A. solid **B.** liquid **C.** gas.

15. sodium at 100 °C

16. copper at 1000 °C

17. sulphur at 600 °C

18. bromine at 0 °C

19. nitrogen at –220 °C

20. chlorine at 0 °C

21. pentane at 50 °C

22. barium chloride at 1000 °C

23. sulphur dioxide at –5 °C

24. magnesium chloride at 500 °C

Fair tests

Questions 1 to 3 refer to the following six experiments which were set up to study the reaction of magnesium with dilute hydrochloric acid.

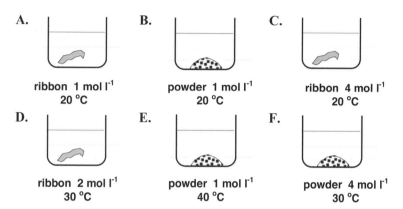

A. ribbon 1 mol l^{-1}
20 °C

B. powder 1 mol l^{-1}
20 °C

C. ribbon 4 mol l^{-1}
20 °C

D. ribbon 2 mol l^{-1}
30 °C

E. powder 1 mol l^{-1}
40 °C

F. powder 4 mol l^{-1}
30 °C

1. Which **two** experiments could be used to show the effect of temperature on the rate of this reaction?

2. Which **two** experiments could be used to show the effect of concentration on the rate of this reaction?

3. Which **two** experiments could be used to show the effect of particle size on the rate of this reaction?

4. Jim was asked to find out whether fertilisers containing potassium ions, K$^+$, or fertilisers containing ammonium ions, NH$_4^+$, are better for growing lettuces.

    He made up two fertiliser solutions for his experiment.

    Which **two** solutions could Jim have used for a fair test?

    A. KNO$_3$
    concentration 1 mol l^{-1}

    B. K$_2$SO$_4$
    concentration 1 mol l^{-1}

    C. K$_2$SO$_4$
    concentration 2 mol l^{-1}

    D. NH$_4$Cl
    concentration 1 mol l^{-1}

    E. (NH$_4$)$_2$SO$_4$
    concentration 1 mol l^{-1}

    F. NH$_4$NO$_3$
    concentration 2 mol l^{-1}

5. Hydrogen is produced by the electrolysis of sodium chloride solution. Six experiments were carried out.

	Concentration of solution / mol l^{-1}	Type of electrode	Voltage / V
A.	1.0	carbon	2.0
B.	2.0	platinum	4.0
C.	2.0	carbon	2.0
D.	2.0	platinum	2.0
E.	1.0	platinum	4.0
F.	4.0	carbon	4.0

Which **two** cells could be compared to investigate whether the voltage affects the volume of hydrogen produced?

Questions 6 and 7 refer to the following six experiments which were set up to study the reactions of magnesium and iron with dilute hydrochloric acid.

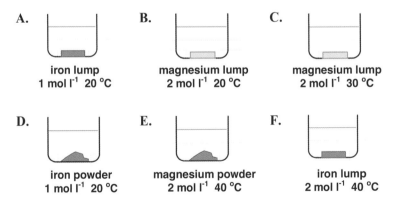

A. iron lump
1 mol l^{-1} 20 °C

B. magnesium lump
2 mol l^{-1} 20 °C

C. magnesium lump
2 mol l^{-1} 30 °C

D. iron powder
1 mol l^{-1} 20 °C

E. magnesium powder
2 mol l^{-1} 40 °C

F. iron lump
2 mol l^{-1} 40 °C

6. Which **two** experiments could be used to investigate the effect of temperature on the rate of reaction?

7. Which **two** experiments could be used to investigate the effect of particle size on the rate of reaction?

Questions 8 and 9 refer to an investigation involving cells.

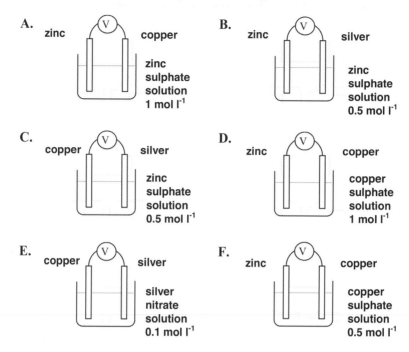

A. zinc — V — copper
zinc sulphate solution 1 mol l⁻¹

B. zinc — V — silver
zinc sulphate solution 0.5 mol l⁻¹

C. copper — V — silver
zinc sulphate solution 0.5 mol l⁻¹

D. zinc — V — copper
copper sulphate solution 1 mol l⁻¹

E. copper — V — silver
silver nitrate solution 0.1 mol l⁻¹

F. zinc — V — copper
copper sulphate solution 0.5 mol l⁻¹

8.　Which **two** cells could be compared to investigate whether the concentration of the electrolyte affects the cell voltage?

9.　Which **two** cells could be compared to investigate whether the type of the electrolyte affects the cell voltage?

10. You have been asked to investigate whether vanadium or chromium is higher in the electrochemical series.

Which **two** cells could be compared to give this information?

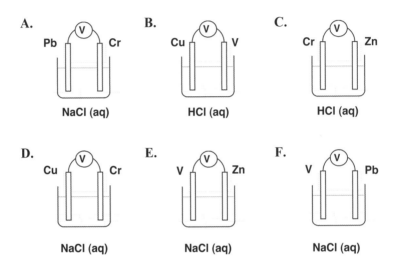

A.
Pb   Cr
NaCl (aq)

B.
Cu   V
HCl (aq)

C.
Cr   Zn
HCl (aq)

D.
Cu   Cr
NaCl (aq)

E.
V   Zn
NaCl (aq)

F.
V   Pb
NaCl (aq)

11. A student compared the effect of dissolving two solids on the boiling point of water.

He added potassium nitrate to water and found the boiling point.
He repeated his experiment using sodium nitrate .

He then compared his results.

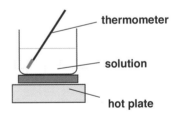

thermometer

solution

hot plate

Which variable had to be the same for both experiments to make the comparison fair?

A. starting temperature of the solution

B. temperature of the laboratory

C. concentration of the solution

D. size of the beake

12. Different brands of antifreeze were compared. A solution of each antifreeze was made and the freezing point was measured .

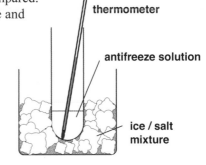

To ensure that comparison of freezing point was fair, which variable had to be the same for all experiments?

A. size of test tube   **B.** concentration of solution

C. volume of solution   **D.** initial temperature of solution

13. A group of students carried out a project on shells – egg shells, snail shells and sea shells.

To compare the mass of calcium carbonate in the different shells, they added each shell sample separately to hydrochloric acid.

They used an excess of hydrochloric acid to make sure all the calcium carbonate in each sample had reacted.

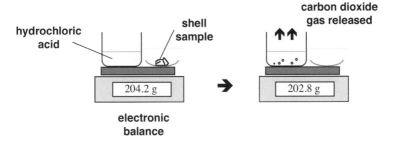

Which factor would most likely be kept the same when comparing the mass of calcium carbonate in the different shells?

A. mass of shell samples   **B.** volume of acid

C. concentration of acid   **D.** particle size of shell samples

Planning and procedures

1. Which apparatus would be most suitable for removing a soluble gas from a mixture of gases?

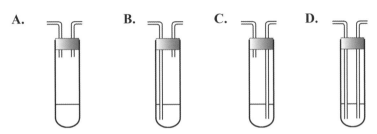

Questions 2 to 4 refer to methods of collecting gases.

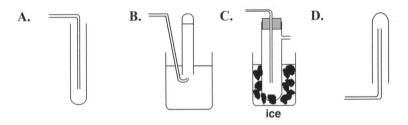

The table shows the information that is known.

	Sulphur dioxide	Ammonia	Hydrogen
Solubility in water	soluble	soluble	insoluble
Density compared to air	more dense	less dense	less dense
Boiling point	-10 °C	-33 °C	-253 °C

2. Which is the best method for collecting sulphur dioxide?

3. Which is the best method for collecting ammonia?

4. Which is the best method for collecting hydrogen?

5. A student was asked to find the mass of copper in a sample of copper oxide.

The student decided to change the oxide to copper metal, and measure the loss in mass.

The apparatus, as it would appear half-way through the experiment, is shown.

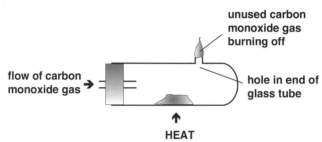

All of the following steps, **not** in the correct order, are used in the experiment.

A. Start the flow of carbon monoxide, light it at the hole, begin heating.

B. Weigh the glass tube and copper.

C. Weigh the glass tube and copper oxide.

D. Continue heating until all copper oxide has been changed to copper.

E. Stop heating, then 5 minutes later, stop the flow of carbon monoxide gas.

F. Weigh the glass tube empty.

Write down the letters for **all** the steps **in the correct order**.

6. A student found the formula for magnesium oxide by the following experimental method.

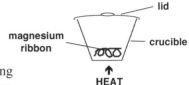

He made magnesium oxide by burning magnesium using the apparatus shown.

By measuring the change in mass, he was able to work out the masses of magnesium and oxygen in the sample of the compound.

All of the following steps, **not** in the correct order, are used in the experiment.

A. Weigh the crucible, lid and magnesium ribbon.

B. Clean the magnesium ribbon with emery paper.

C. Stop heating and allow crucible and contents to cool.

D. Weigh the crucible, lid and magnesium oxide.

E. Weigh the empty crucible and lid.

F. Heat the magnesium ribbon in the crucible.

Write down the letters for **all** the steps **in the correct order**.

7.

    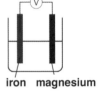

| iron | tin | iron | copper | iron | zinc | iron | magnesium |

In order to place the metals in order of ability to supply electrons it is necessary to set up two more cells.

What two pairs are required?

A. tin/copper and magnesium/zinc

B. tin/magnesium and zinc/copper

C. tin/zinc and magnesium/copper

D. tin/zinc and zinc/copper.

Drawing conclusions (i)

Questions 1 and 2 refer to the properties of five different elements.

Element **A.**	solid	metal	conducts electricity
Element **B.**	liquid	metal	conducts electricity
Element **C.**	solid	non-metal	does not conduct electricity
Element **D.**	solid	metal	conducts electricity
Element **E.**	solid	non-metal	conducts electricity

1. Which element could be carbon in the form of graphite?

2. The properties of which **two** elements do **not** support the view that only metallic solids conduct electricity?

Questions 3 to 8 refer to the burning of a solid compound in air.

Large amounts of sulphur dioxide, and nitrogen were found to be the only two gases in the mixture present after burning.

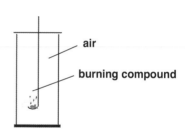

For each of the following possible statements about the results, **on the evidence from the results alone**, decide whether the statement

    A. must be true   **B. could** be true   **C.** can **NOT** be true.

3. The compound contained sulphur.

4. The compound contained oxygen.

5. The compound contained nitrogen.

6. The compound contained carbon and sulphur.

7. The compound contained carbon but **not** sulphur.

8. The compound contained sulphur but **not** nitrogen.

Questions 9 to 14 refer to an experiment in which Bill heated an unknown substance with copper oxide.

He found that only copper, water and carbon dioxide were formed.

For each of the following possible statements about the results, **on the evidence from the results alone**, decide whether the statement

      A. must be true   **B. could** be true   **C. ** can **NOT** be true.

9.   The substance contains carbon.

10.   The substance contains oxygen.

11.   The substance contains hydrogen.

12.   The substance contains copper, carbon and oxygen only.

13.   The substance is a carbohydrate.

14.   The substance is copper carbonate.

Questions 15 to 18 refer to the following experiment. It was carried out to estimate the percentage of oxygen in the air.

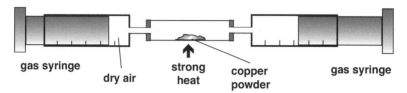

gas syringe

dry air

strong heat

copper powder

gas syringe

A 100 cm^3 sample of dry air was put into the left hand syringe. The copper was then heated and the air was passed back and forth from one syringe to the other. The hot copper reacts with the oxygen.

After some time, the heat was removed and the apparatus was allowed to cool. The volume of gas left in the syringes was 85 cm^3.

Decide whether each of the following statements

    A.   could be used to explain this result

    B.   could **NOT** be used to explain this result.

15.   Heating was stopped too soon.

16.   The air was passed back and forward for too long.

17.   Not enough copper powder was used.

18.   The air has more than the normal amount of oxygen.

Questions 19 to 24 refer to the following experiment. It was carried out to find the formula of a powdered substance in a bottle labelled 'copper oxide'.

The student reduced the copper oxide to copper metal, and measured the change in mass. This allowed the masses of copper and oxygen in the compound to be worked out.

The apparatus, as it would appear half-way through the experiment, is shown.

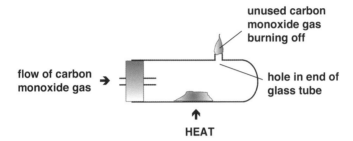

It was calculated that copper(I) oxide, Cu_2O, would lose 11% of its mass and copper(II) oxide, CuO, would lose 20% of its mass. The measured mass loss was 15%.

Decide whether each of the following statements

    A.   could be used to explain this result

    B.   could **NOT** be used to explain this result.

19.   The powder was copper(I) oxide; heating went on too long.

20.   The powder was copper(I) oxide; it was damp before it was heated.

21.   The powder was a mixture of copper(I) oxide and copper(II) oxide.

22.   The powder was copper(I) oxide; heating was stopped too soon.

23.   The powder was copper(II) oxide; carbon monoxide flow was stopped too soon.

24.   The powder was copper(II) oxide; the carbon monoxide flow was continued for too long.

Drawing conclusions (ii)

Questions 1 to 4 refer to the characteristic flame colours of ions.

Different compounds were heated at the end of a rod and the resulting flame colours are shown in the table.

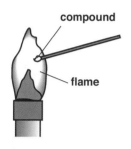

compound

flame

Compound	Flame colour
sodium chloride	yellow
copper(II) chloride	blue-green
potassium chloride	lilac
sodium sulphate	yellow
copper(II) sulphate	blue-green
potassium sulphate	lilac

Decide whether each of the following statements is

A.   TRUE   B.   FALSE.

1.   A compound containing copper(II) ions gives blue-green flames.

2.   The lilac flame of potassium sulphate is due to the potassium ion.

3.   Sulphate ions do not give a colour to the flames.

4.   The yellow flame of sodium chloride is due to the chloride ion.

Questions 5 to 10 refer to a process called extraction.

Extraction means obtaining a pure metal from one of its compounds.

Decide whether each of the following equations

   A.   represents the extraction of a metal

   B.   does **NOT** represent the extraction of a metal.

5. $Zn\,(s)$ + $H_2O\,(g)$ → $ZnO\,(s)$ + $H_2\,(g)$

6. $SnO_2\,(s)$ + $C\,(s)$ → $Sn\,(l)$ + $CO_2\,(g)$

7. $CaCl_2\,(l)$ → $Ca\,(s)$ + $Cl_2\,(g)$

8. $Ni\,(s)$ + $2HC\,l(aq)$ → $NiCl_2\,(aq)$ + $H_2\,(g)$

9. $2Ba\,(s)$ + $O_2\,(g)$ → $2BaO\,(s)$

10. $FeO\,(s)$ + $CO\,(g)$ → $Fe\,(s)$ + $CO_2\,(g)$

Questions 11 to 16 refer to hard water, i.e. water which forms a scum when soap is added to it.

In an experiment to find out which ions make water hard, soap was added to various solutions.

The results of the experiments are shown in the table.

Compound	Does a scum form?
sodium chloride	no
sodium nitrate	no
magnesium chloride	yes
sodium sulphate	no
iron(II) sulphate	yes
magnesium nitrate	yes

Decide whether each of the following ions

    A.   makes water hard   **B.**   does **NOT** make water hard.

11.   iron(II) ion

12.   magnesium ion

13.   sodium ion

14.   chloride ion

15.   nitrate ion

16.   sulphate ion

Questions 17 to 20 refer to the graph which shows how the solubilities of three salts vary with temperature.

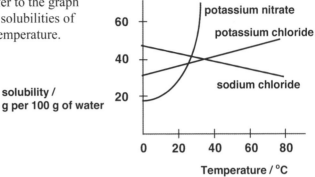

Decide whether each of the following statements is

A. TRUE **B.** FALSE.

17. At 10 °C potassium nitrate is more soluble than sodium chloride.

18. At 20 °C sodium chloride is more soluble than potassium chloride.

19. At 40 °C potassium chloride is more soluble than potassium nitrate.

20. At 50 °C sodium chloride is more soluble than potassium nitrate.

Questions 21 to 26 refer to alkanals and alkanones, two families of carbon compounds, each having the same general formula $C_nH_{2n}O$.

The two families differ because only the alkanals contain the following arrangement of atoms.

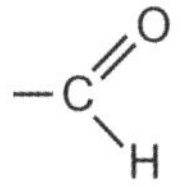

Decide whether each of the following structural formulae could represent

    A.   an alkanal

    B.   an alkanone

    C.   **neither** an alkanal **nor** an alkanone.

21.

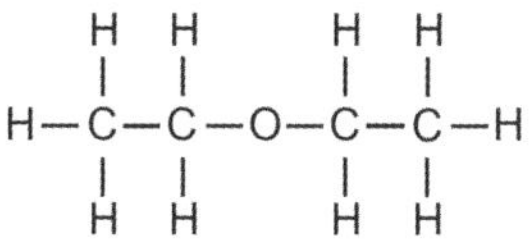

22.

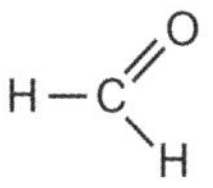

23.

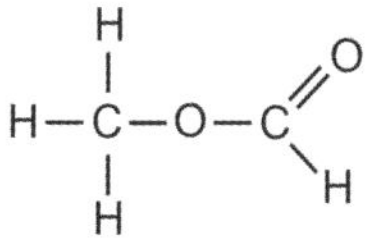

24.

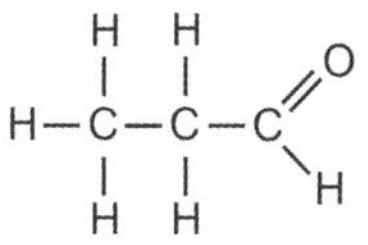

25.

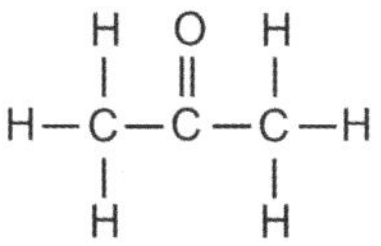

26.

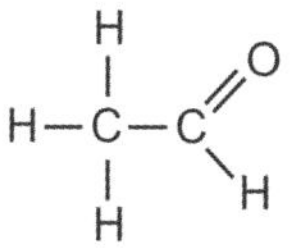

Questions 27 to 32 refer to compounds which contain hydrogen bonds.

Hydrogen bonds exist between molecules if the molecules contain a hydrogen atom directly bonded to a nitrogen or oxygen or fluorine atom.

Decide whether each of the following compounds

     A.   has hydrogen bonds between its molecules

     B.   does **NOT** have hydrogen bonds between its molecules.

27.   H—N with H and H branches

30.   H—F

28.   H—C—O—H (with H above and below the C)

31.   H—C—N structure with CH₃ groups

29.   F—N with F and F branches

32.   H—C—O—C—H (with H above and below each C)

Questions 33 and 34 refer to alkanones and alkanoic acids, two families of carbon compounds.

Each family has a particular arrangement of atoms.

□ represents the rest of the molecule

Alkanones can be prepared from alkanoic acids.

$$CH_3\!-\!\overset{\overset{\displaystyle O}{\|}}{C}\!-\!OH \quad + \quad C_2H_5\!-\!\overset{\overset{\displaystyle O}{\|}}{C}\!-\!OH \quad \rightarrow \quad CH_3\!-\!\overset{\overset{\displaystyle O}{\|}}{C}\!-\!C_2H_5 \quad + \quad CO_2 \quad + \quad H_2O$$

The structural formulae for some alkanones are:

A. $C_2H_5\!-\!\overset{\overset{\displaystyle O}{\|}}{C}\!-\!C_3H_7$

B. $C_2H_5\!-\!\overset{\overset{\displaystyle O}{\|}}{C}\!-\!C_4H_9$

C. $C_3H_7\!-\!\overset{\overset{\displaystyle O}{\|}}{C}\!-\!C_3H_7$

D. $C_3H_7\!-\!\overset{\overset{\displaystyle O}{\|}}{C}\!-\!C_4H_9$

33.   Which alkanone can be produced from a mixture of the following alkanoic acids?

$$C_2H_5\!-\!\overset{\overset{\displaystyle O}{\|}}{C}\!-\!OH \quad \text{and} \quad C_4H_9\!-\!\overset{\overset{\displaystyle O}{\|}}{C}\!-\!OH$$

34.   Which alkanone can be prepared from only **one** alkanoic acid?

Questions 35 to 44 refer to hydration and dehydration reactions.

Hydration is the addition of the elements from water to a single compound; dehydration is the removal of the elements to make water from a single compound.

Decide whether each of the following reactions is

    A.   a hydration reaction

    B.   a dehydration reaction

    C.   **neither** a hydration **nor** a dehydration reaction.

35. C_2H_4 + H_2O → C_2H_5OH

36. CH_4 + $2O_2$ → CO_2 + $2H_2O$

37. $C_6H_{12}O_6$ →   6C   + $6H_2O$

38. $2H_2$ + O_2 → $2H_2O$

39. C_2H_2 + H_2O → C_2H_4O

40. HNO_3 +   KOH   → KNO_3 + H_2O

41. $3Al(OH)_3$ → Al_2O_3 + $3H_2O$

42.   Ca   + $2H_2O$ → $Ca(OH)_2$ + H_2

43. C_3H_7OH → C_3H_6 + H_2O

44.   CuO   + H_2 →   Cu   + H_2O

Chemical Changes and Structure

Test 1		Test 2		Test 3		Test 4		Test 5				Test 6	
1.	A	1.	C	1.	A	1.	A	1.	A	21.	A	1.	C
2.	B	2.	A	2.	A	2.	A	2.	B	22.	B	2.	B
3.	B	3.	B	3.	B	3.	B	3.	A	23.	C	3.	C
4.	B	4.	D	4.	A	4.	A	4.	B	24.	C	4.	C
5.	B	5.	C	5.	A	5.	B	5.	A	25.	A	5.	A
6.	A	6.	C	6.	B	6.	A	6.	A	26.	C	6.	B
7.	B	7.	D	7.	A	7.	B	7.	B	27.	B	7.	B
8.	B	8.	A	8.	A	8.	A	8.	A	28.	B	8.	A
9.	A	9.	C	9.	C	9.	C	9.	A	29.	C	9.	C
10.	A	10.	B			10.	B	10.	A	30.	A	10.	B
						11.	A	11.	B	31.	B	11.	D
						12.	D	12.	A	32.	B	12.	C
						13.	C	13.	C	33.	B	13.	B
						14.	B	14.	A	34.	C	14.	A
								15.	A	35.	A	15.	B
								16.	C	36.	B	16.	A
								17.	A	37.	A	17.	A
								18.	A	38.	A	18.	B
								19.	C	39.	A	19.	A
								20.	B	40.	B	20.	B
												21.	A
												22.	B
												23.	B
												24.	A

Test 7

1. A
2. E
3. D
4. C
5. B
6. A
7. E
8. C
9. D
10. B
11. D
12. A
13. E
14. C
15. B
16. D
17. E
18. D
19. C
20. E

Test 8

1. A
2. A
3. B
4. B
5. B
6. A
7. A
8. B
9. B
10. B
11. A
12. B
13. C
14. A
15. B
16. A
17. C
18. C

Test 9

1. copper chloride
2. sodium oxide
3. iron bromide
4. lead sulphide
5. hydrogen iodide
6. magnesium nitride
7. hydrogen and oxygen
8. copper, sulphur and oxygen
9. calcium and nitrogen
10. sodium, carbon and oxygen
11. nitrogen and hydrogen
12. carbon and chlorine
13. sodium and sulphur
14. calcium, sulphur and oxygen
15. potassium, nitrogen and oxygen
16. aluminium and bromine
17. sodium, phosphorus and oxygen
18. potassium, chromium and oxygen

Test 10

1. A
2. C
3. B
4. C
5. B
6. B
7. B
8. C
9. D
10. D

Test 11

1. D
2. B
3. C
4. B
5. C
6. A
7. D
8. A
9. D
10. C
11. B
12. B
13. D
14. A
15. C
16. D
17. A
18. C
19. B

Test 12	Test 13	Test 14	Test 15	Test 16	Test 17	Test 18
1. B	1. B	1. B	1. B	1. A	1. B	1. A
2. C	2. A	2. B	2. A	2. B	2. A	2. C
3. C	3. C	3. A	3. A	3. A	3. B	3. B
4. B	4. A	4. B	4. A	4. A	4. C	4. B
5. C	5. D	5. A	5. B	5. B	5. A	5. A
6. B	6. B	6. D	6. B	6. A		6. C
7. A	7. A	7. B	7. B	7. A		7. B
8. C	8. A	8. B	8. A	8. B		8. A
9. B	9. B	9. B	9. B	9. A		9. A
10. C	10. A		10. A	10. A		10. B
11. A	11. B		11. B			11. A
12. B	12. B		12. B			12. B
13. A	13. D					13. B
14. B	14. B					14. A
15. B						
16. D						
17. B						

Test 19	Test 20	Test 21	Test 22	Test 23	Test 24
1. B	1. C	1. CH_4	1. H_2O	1. KCl	1. $NaNO_3$
2. A	2. D	2. Cl_2	2. HCl	2. $MgBr_2$	2. LiOH
3. B	3. A	3. NH_3	3. NH_3	3. CaO	3. $BaSO_4$
4. A	4. B	4. C_4H_8O	4. CF_4	4. Na_2S	4. $KHCO_3$
5. B	5. A	5. HF	5. PCl_3	5. Mg_3N_2	5. Na_3PO_4
6. A	6. E	6. Si_2H_6	6. SiO_2	6. $RaCl_2$	6. $Ca(NO_3)_2$
7. B	7. B	7. C_2H_4O	7. $SeBr_2$	7. AlF_3	7. KOH
8. A	8. A	8. CS_2	8. SI_2	8. Al_2O_3	8. $Al_2(SO_4)_3$
9. B	9. C	9. $SiCl_4$	9. NO_2	9. LiBr	9. $CaCO_3$
10. A	10. E	10. C_2H_6O	10. CO	10. CsF	10. NH_4Cl
11. A	11. A	11. B F G H	11. SO_3		11. $Mg(OH)_2$
12. B	12. B	12. A B F G	12. CBr_4		12. $Ca(HSO_4)_2$
13. A	13. A	13. E	13. CO_2		13. $LiHCO_3$
14. B	14. D	14. C	14. UF_6		14. $(NH_4)_3PO_4$
15. B		15. A			15. $Al(NO_3)_3$
16. B		16. F			16. Na_2CO_3
17. C		17. D			17. K_2SO_4
18. B		18. B			18. $Ba(OH)_2$
19. C		19. G			19. $(NH_4)_2CO_3$
20. C					20. $Ra(HSO_4)_2$
21. A					
22. D					

Chemical Changes and Structure - answers

Test 25	Test 26	Test 27	Test 28	Test 29	Test 30
1. CuCl	1. LiCl	1. A	1. B	1. B	1. B
2. FeO	2. Mg(NO$_3$)$_2$	2. B	2. B	2. B	2. A
3. Fe$_2$S$_3$	3. N$_2$	3. A	3. A	3. B	3. A
4. CuBr$_2$	4. KOH	4. A	4. B	4. A	4. B
5. SnO$_2$	5. NH$_4$Br	5. B	5. A	5. A	5. B
6. NiCO$_3$	6. RbF	6. B	6. A	6. A	6. A
7. Pb(NO$_3$)$_2$	7. MgSO$_4$	7. A	7. B	7. C	7. B
8. FeBr$_2$	8. Sn	8. A	8. B	8. A	8. A
9. V$_2$O$_5$	9. Na$_2$S	9. B	9. B	9. B	9. B
10. Co(OH)$_3$	10. CO	10. A	10. B	10 C	10. B
	11. HCl	11. A	11. B	11. A	11. A
	12. FeCl$_3$	12. B	12. A	12. D	12. C
	13. Ca		13. B	13. C	13. D
	14. Br$_2$		14. B	14. B	14. C
	15. SrCl$_2$		15. B		15. D
	16. (NH$_4$)$_2$CO$_3$		16. B		16. A
	17. Fe(OH)$_2$		17. C		17. B
	18. HI		18. A		18. D
	19. SO$_3$		19. C		19. A
	20. MgS		20. B		20. B
			21. A		21. B
			22. C		22. A
			23. A		23. B

Test 31

1. petrol + oxygen ➔ carbon dioxide + water
2. starch + water ➔ glucose
3. carbon monoxide + oxygen ➔ carbon dioxide
4. carbon dioxide + water ➔ glucose + oxygen
5. iron oxide + carbon monoxide ➔ iron + carbon dioxide
6. ethene + hydrogen ➔ ethane
7. silver nitrate + sodium chloride ➔ silver chloride + sodium nitrate
8. hydrogen peroxide ➔ water + oxygen
9. zinc + hydrochloric acid ➔ zinc chloride + hydrogen
10. copper carbonate ➔ copper oxide + carbon dioxide

Test 32

1. Carbon reacts with oxygen to form carbon dioxide.
2. Carbon monoxide reacts with oxygen (burns) to form carbon dioxide.
3. Zinc reacts with chlorine to form zinc chloride.
4. Silicon reacts with bromine to form silicon tetrabromide.
5. Sulphur dioxide reacts with oxygen to form sulphur trioxide.
6. Nitrogen hydride (ammonia) decomposes to form nitrogen and hydrogen.
7. Sodium reacts with fluorine to form sodium fluoride.
8. Iron reacts with sulphur to form iron sulphide.
9. Copper oxide reacts with hydrogen to form copper and water.
10. Silver nitrate solution reacts with dilute hydrochloric acid to form solid silver chloride and dilute nitric acid.
11. Magnesium reacts with dilute sulphuric acid to form magnesium sulphate and hydrogen .
12. Copper carbonate decomposes to form copper oxide and carbon dioxide .
13. Ammonium chloride reacts with sodium hydroxide to form sodium chloride, water and nitrogen hydride (ammonia).
14. Magnesium reacts with nitrogen to form magnesium nitride .
15. Potassium carbonate solution reacts with barium chloride solution to form potassium chloride solution and solid barium carbonate .

Test 33

1. C + O_2 → CO_2
2. $2Na$ + Cl_2 → $2NaCl$
3. C + $2Br_2$ → CBr_4
4. C_2H_4 + $3O_2$ → $2CO_2$ + $2H_2O$
5. $2H_2O_2$ → $2H_2O$ + O_2
6. Mg + $2AgNO_3$ → $Mg(NO_3)_2$ + $2Ag$
7. $2NaOH$ + H_2SO_4 → Na_2SO_4 + $2H_2O$
8. $2AgNO_3$ + $BaCl_2$ → $Ba(NO_3)_2$ + $2AgCl$
9. $2Na$ + $2H_2O$ → $2NaOH$ + H_2
10. $2Al$ + $3Cl_2$ → $2AlCl_3$
11. $2KI$ + H_2O + O_3 → $2KOH$ + O_2 + I_2
12. $2C_3H_8O_3$ → $3CO_2$ + $3CH_4$ + $2H_2$
13. Al_4C_3 + $12H_2O$ → $4Al(OH)_3$ + $3CH_4$
14. $2B_2O_3$ + $7C$ → B_4C + $6CO$
15. $4NH_3$ + $5O_2$ → $4NO$ + $6H_2O$
16. $4C_3H_5N_3O_9$ → $6N_2$ + $10H_2O$ + $12CO_2$ + $6O_2$

Test 34

1. $2C$ + O_2 → $2CO$
2. $2SO_2$ + O_2 → $2SO_3$
3. $2HCl$ → H_2 + Cl_2
4. $2H_2$ + O_2 → $2H_2O$
5. $2P$ + $3Cl_2$ → $2PCl_3$
6. Si + $2F_2$ → SiF_4
7. CH_4 + $2O_2$ → CO_2 + $2H_2O$
8. C + $2Cl_2$ → CCl_4
9. N_2 + $2O_2$ → $2NO_2$
10. $4NH_3$ + $3O_2$ → $2N_2$ + $6H_2O$
11. S + O_2 → SO_2
12. Si + $2Cl_2$ → $SiCl_4$
13. C_2H_4 + $3O_2$ → $2CO_2$ + $2H_2O$
14. H_2 + I_2 → $2HI$
15. $2NH_3$ → N_2 + $3H_2$

Chemical Changes and Structure - answers

Test 35

1.	2Mg	+	O_2	→	2MgO				
2.	2K	+	Cl_2	→	2KCl				
3.	Ca	+	$H_2SO_4(aq)$	→	$CaSO_4$	+	H_2		
4.	2Mg	+	SO_2	→	2MgO	+	S		
5.	$BaCl_2(aq)$	+	$Na_2SO_4(aq)$	→	2NaCl(aq)	+	$BaSO_4(s)$		
6.	2Li	+	2HCl(aq)	→	2LiCl	+	H_2		
7.	Na_2CO_3	+	$2HNO_3(aq)$	→	$2NaNO_3$	+	CO_2	+	H_2O
8.	Na_2O	+	$H_2SO_4(aq)$	→	Na_2SO_4	+	H_2O		
9.	2Fe	+	O_2	→	2FeO				
10.	Ca	+	$2H_2O$	→	$Ca(OH)_2$	+	H_2		
11.	$Mg(OH)_2$	+	$2HNO_3(aq)$	→	$Mg(NO_3)_2$	+	$2H_2O$		
12.	$2NH_3$	+	$H_2SO_4(aq)$	→	$(NH_4)_2SO_4$				
13.	$Pb(NO_3)_2(aq)$	+	2KCl(aq)	→	$PbCl_2(s)$	+	$2KNO_3(aq)$		
14.	2Li	+	Cl_2	→	2LiCl				
15.	2Al	+	$3F_2$	→	$2AlF_3$				
16.	2Na	+	Br_2	→	2NaBr				
17.	4Al	+	$3O_2$	→	$2Al_2O_3$				

Test 36

1. barium chloride solution + sodium sulphate solution
   → sodium chloride solution + barium sulphate
   $BaCl_2$ (aq) + Na_2SO_4 (aq) → 2NaCl (aq) + $BaSO_4$ (s)

2. sodium carbonate solution + calcium chloride solution
   → sodium chloride solution + calcium carbonate
   Na_2CO_3 (aq) + $CaCl_2$ (aq) → 2NaCl (aq) + $CaCO_3$ (s)

3. silver nitrate solution + lithium chloride solution
   → lithium nitrate solution + silver chloride
   $AgNO_3$ (aq) + LiCl (aq) → $LiNO_3$ (aq) + AgCl (s)

4. lead chloride solution + sodium iodide solution
   → sodium chloride solution + lead iodide
   $PbCl_2$ (aq) + 2NaI (aq) → 2NaCl (aq) + PbI_2 (s)

5. lead(II) nitrate solution + sodium chloride solution
   → sodium nitrate solution + lead(II) chloride
   $Pb(NO_3)_2$ (aq) + 2NaCl (aq) → $2NaNO_3$ (aq) + $PbCl_2$ (s)

6. sodium hydroxide solution + lead(II) nitrate solution
   → sodium nitrate solution + lead(II) hydroxide
   2NaOH (aq) + $Pb(NO_3)_2$ (aq) → $2NaNO_3$ (aq) + $Pb(OH)_2$ (s)

7. calcium nitrate solution + potassium carbonate solution
   → potassium nitrate solution + calcium carbonate
   $Ca(NO_3)_2$ (aq) + K_2CO_3 (aq) → $2KNO_3$ (aq) + $CaCO_3$ (s)

8. tin(II) chloride solution + barium hydroxide solution
   → barium chloride solution + tin(II) hydroxide
   $SnCl_2$ (aq) + $Ba(OH)_2$ (aq) → $BaCl_2$ (aq) + $Sn(OH)_2$ (s)

Test 37	Test 38		Test 39	Test 40
1. 44	1. 80 g	21. 0.25	1. 0.5 mol	1. 4 g
2. 101.5	2. 58.5 g	22. 2.2	2. 0.1 mol	2. 2.8 g
3. 30	3. 12 g	23. 0.2	3. 0.01 mol	3. 10.6 g
4. 136	4. 132 g	24. 0.2	4. 0.5 mol	4. 0.345 g
5. 160	5. 46 g	25. 0.1	5. 0.4 mol	5. 0.1 mol l^{-1}
6. 164	6. 120.5 g	26. 0.2	6. 10 mol l^{-1}	6. 0.1 mol l^{-1}
7. 78	7. 28 g	27. 2	7. 2.5 mol l^{-1}	7. 0.8 mol l^{-1}
8. 58	8. 79.5 g	28. 0.1	8. 0.2 mol l^{-1}	8. 0.4 mol l^{-1}
9. 64	9. 148.5 g	29. 0.04	9. 0.8 mol l^{-1}	9. 2.5 mol l^{-1}
10. 102	10. 234 g	30. 2	10. 2 mol l^{-1}	10. 4.2 g
11. 2	11. 127 g	31. B	11. 0.2 l (200 cm^3)	11. 53 g
12. 107	12. 2.8 g	32. A	12. 2 l	12. 0.08 mol l^{-1}
13. 106	13. 48 g	33. A	13. 0.05 l (50 cm^3)	
14. 96	14. 111 g	34. C	14. 5 l	
15. 28	15. 320 g	35. D	15. 0.25 l (250 cm^3)	
16. 164	16. 284 g			
	17. 125 g			
	18. 56.5 g			
	19. 435 g			
	20. 1.6 g			

Test 41		Test 42	Test 43	Test 44
1. C	21. B	1. A	1. A	1. A
2. A	22. A	2. B	2. B	2. B
3. C	23. B	3. B	3. A	3. A
4. B	24. B	4. A	4. C	4. B
5. A	25. B	5. A	5. B	5. A
6. B		6. B	6. B	6. B
7. A		7. A	7. B	7. A
8. A		8. B	8. C	8. A
9. A		9. B	9. A	9. B
10. A		10. B	10. C	10. A
11. A		11. A	11. A	11. B
12. C		12. A	12. B	12. A
13. A		13. B		13. B
14. B				14. B
15. A				15. B
16. B				16. B
17. B				17. A
18. A				18. B
19. A				19. A
20. B				20. B

Test 45	Test 46	Test 47	Test 48	Test 49
1. B	1. B	1. B	1. 100 cm^3	1. B
2. A	2. A	2. A	2. 40 cm^3	2. A
3. B	3. A	3. C	3. 0.1 mol l^{-1}	3. A
4. B	4. B	4. A	4. 25 cm^3	4. B
5. A	5. B	5. A	5. 0.5 mol l^{-1}	5. A
6. A	6. B	6. C	6. 50 cm^3	6. B
7. B	7. A	7. C	7. 0.127 mol l^{-1}	7. B
8. A	8. B	8. B	8. 44 cm^3	8. A
9. B	9. A		9. 16.7 cm^3	9. B
10. B	10. B		10. 0.156 mol l^{-1}	10. A
11. A				11. E
12. B				12. D F
13. B				13. A
14. A				14. B
15. C				15. B
16. B				16. B
17. A				17. A
18. C				18. A
19. A				
20. B				
21. A				
22. C				
23. A				

Test 50

1. B	21. B E
2. A	22. A
3. A	23. B
4. A	24. B
5. A	25. B
6. B	26. B
7. A	27. A
8. A	28. B
9. A	29. B
10. B	30. B
11. B	31. A
12. A B	32. A
13. E	33. B
14. B	34. A
15. A	
16. B	
17. A	
18. B	
19. B	
20. C D	

Nature's Chemistry

Test 1	Test 2		Test 3	Test 4	
1. B	1. B	21. B	1. A D	1. A	21. D
2. D	2. C	22. F	2. B D	2. B	22. C
3. A	3. B	23. C	3. C E	3. A	23. D
4. D	4. C	24. A	4. B D	4. B	
5. D	5. D	25. E	5. A D	5. D	
6. A	6. A	26. D	6. C E	6. A	
7. B	7. B		7. A D	7. C	
8. A	8. A		8. C E	8. B	
9. A	9. B		9. B D	9. C	
10. D	10. A		10. B D	10. A	
11. A	11. B		11. A D	11. C	
12. A	12. A		12. C E	12. C	
13. D	13. A		13. G	13. C	
14. C	14. B		14. H	14. A	
15. B	15. A		15. F	15. D	
16. A	16. A		16. C	16. D	
	17. A		17. A	17. B	
	18. B		18. E	18. C	
	19. A			19. A	
	20. A			20. C	

Test 5

1. 2,3-dimethylbutane
2. pent-1-ene
3. 4-methylpent-2-ene
4. 2-methylpentane
5. 2-methylbut-1-ene
6. 3,4-dimethylpent-2-ene
7. 3-ethylpentane
   Note: number not required
8. 4-methylpent-1-ene
9. 2,2-dimethylbutane
10. 3-methylpentane
11. cyclohexene
12. methylcyclohexane

Test 6	Test 7	Test 8	
1. B	1. B	1. B	21. B
2. A	2. A	2. A	22. A
3. B	3. B	3. B	23. A
4. B	4. A	4. A	24. B
5. B	5. A	5. B	25. B
6. A	6. A	6. A	26. B
7. B	7. A	7. B	27. C
8. A	8. A	8. A	28. C
9. A	9. B	9. A	29. B
10. B	10. A	10. B	30. A
11. B	11. A	11. B	31. B
12. B	12. B	12. B	32. B
13. A	13. C	13. B	
14. A	14. D	14. A	
15. B	15. A	15. B	
16. B		16. A	
17. A		17. B	
18. B		18. A	
19. A		19. B	
20. A		20. A	
21. A			
22. B			

Test 9	Test 10	Test 11	Test 12	Test 13
1. C	1. A	1. A	1. C F L	1. methanol
2. A	2. A	2. A	2. B G K	2. ethanoic acid
3. B	3. A	3. B	3. D E H	3. propan-1-ol
4. A	4. A	4. A		4. methanoic acid
5. B	5. B	5. B		5. ethanol
6. B	6. A	6. A		6. butanoic acid
7. B	7. A	7. A		7. A
8. B	8. A	8. B		8. B
9. C	9. B	9. A		9. A
10. A	10. B	10. A		10. B
11. C	11. B	11. B		11. methyl ethanoate
	12. A	12. A		12. propyl ethanoate
		13. B		13. ethyl methanoate
		14. A		14. methyl methanoate
				15. D
				16. B
				17. C
				18. A

Test 14	Test 15	Test 16	Test 17
1. B	1. 4.18 kJ	1. 4.4 g	1. A
2. A	2. 3.55 kJ	2. 9 g	2. B D
3. B	3. 6.69 kJ	3. 159 g	3. B D
4. A	4. 5.94 kJ	4. 9 g	4. B
5. A	5. 8.82 kJ	5. 2.8 g	5. A
6. B	6. 6.19 kJ	6. 22 g	6. D
7. B	7. 1.55 kJ	7. 0.2 g	7. D
8. A	8. 21.9 kJ	8. 0.4 g	8. C
9. A		9. 4 g	9. A B
10. B		10. 7.33 g	10. A
11. B			11. B
12. A			12. A
13. A			13. B
14. B			14. A

Chemistry in Society

Test 1

1.	B	21.	C
2.	D	22.	A
3.	A	23.	B
4.	C	24.	B
5.	B	25.	B
6.	A	26.	A
7.	A	27.	A
8.	A	28.	B
9.	B		
10.	B		
11.	A		
12.	B		
13.	B		
14.	B		
15.	A		
16.	B		
17.	B		
18.	A		
19.	D		
20.	B		

Test 2

1.	B
2.	A
3.	B
4.	A
5.	B
6.	B
7.	A
8.	A
9.	B
10.	A
11.	B
12.	A
13.	B
14.	A
15.	B

Test 3

1.	A
2.	B
3.	A
4.	A
5.	B
6.	B
7.	B
8.	B
9.	A
10.	A

Test 4

1.	A
2.	A
3.	D
4.	D
5.	B
6.	B

Test 5

1.	B
2.	A
3.	B
4.	B
5.	A
6.	B
7.	A
8.	A
9.	B
10.	A
11.	A
12.	B

Test 6

1.	A
2.	B
3.	A
4.	B
5.	A
6.	B
7.	A
8.	B
9.	A
10.	A
11.	B
12.	B
13.	A
14.	B
15.	A
16.	A

Test 7

1.	A	21.	B
2.	A	22.	B
3.	A	23.	A
4.	B	24.	B
5.	A	25.	A
6.	A		
7.	B		
8.	B		
9.	B		
10.	A		
11.	B		
12.	A		
13.	D		
14.	C		
15.	C		
16.	C		
17.	A		
18.	A		
19.	B		
20.	A		

Test 8

1.	A
2.	B
3.	B
4.	A
5.	B
6.	B
7.	B
8.	A
9.	B
10.	B
11.	A
12.	B

Test 9

1.	D	21.	B
2.	C	22.	B
3.	A	23.	A
4.	A	24.	B
5.	B	25.	B
6.	B	26.	C
7.	B	27.	A
8.	B	28.	D
9.	A	29.	C
10.	B	30.	C
11.	B	31.	B
12.	A	32.	B
13.	B	33.	B
14.	B	34.	A
15.	A	35.	D
16.	B	36.	B
17.	B		
18.	B		
19.	A		
20.	A		

Test 10

1.	A
2.	A
3.	B
4.	A
5.	B
6.	A
7.	B
8.	B
9.	C
10.	B
11.	B
12.	B
13.	A
14.	A
15.	B
16.	A

Test 11	Test 12	Test 13	Test 14	Test 15	Test 16			
1. B	1. B	1. A	1. B	1. B	1.	H 11.1%	O 88.9%	
2. B	2. B	2. A	2. B	2. A	2.	C 80%	H 20%	
3. A	3. C	3. B	3. A	3. A	3.	Ca 36%	Cl 64%	
4. A	4. B	4. A	4. A	4. B	4.	Na 57.5%	O 40%	
5. A	5. A	5. A	5. A	5. A		H 2.5%		
6. B	6. C	6. B	6. A	6. B	5.	K 56.5%	C 8.7%	
7. A	7. D	7. A	7. B	7. D		O 34.8%		
8. B	8. D	8. A	8. B		6.	Li 10.1%	N 20.3%	
9. B	9. B	9. A	9. B			O 69.6%		
10. B	10. C	10. A	10. A		7.	C 62.1%	H 10.3%	
11. A		11. B	11. B			O 27.6%		
12. B		12. A	12. A		8.	Al 34.6%	O 61.5%	
13. A		13. A	13. A			H 3.8%		
14. A		14. B	14. B		9.	Fe 36.8%	S 21.1%	
15. A		15. A	15. A			O 42.1%		
16. A			16. A		10.	N 28.2%	H 8.1%	
17. B						P 20.8%	O 43%	
18. A					11. A			
					12. 389.6 g			

Test 17	Test 18		Test 19	Test 20	Test 21
1. B	1. B	21. A	1. B	1. B	1. C E
2. A	2. A	22. C	2. C	2. A	2. D
3. C	3. B	23. D	3. C	3. A	3. C
4. C	4. D	24. A	4. C	4. B	4. A F
5. A	5. B	25. D	5. B	5. A	5. A D
6. B	6. A	26. D	6. B	6. B	6. A D
7. A	7. A		7. D	7. A	7. B
8. C	8. B		8. B	8. B	8. A
9. B	9. B		9. A	9. B	9. A
10. A	10. A		10. C	10. A	10. B
11. C	11. C		11. C	11. A	11. A
12. C	12. B		12. B	12. B	12. B
	13. C			13. B	13. B
	14. B				14. A
	15. A				15. A
	16. C				16. B
	17. C				
	18. B				
	19. A				
	20. C				

Problem solving

Chemical tests	Types of reactions	Using the data booklet		Fair tests	Planning and procedures
1. B	1. A D	1. D	21. C	1. B E	1. B
2. A	2. C	2. C	22. B	2. A C	2. A
3. E	3. B	3. A	23. C	3. A B	3. D
4. F	4. A D	4. C	24. A	4. B E	4. B
5. C	5. B	5. C		5. B D	5. FCADEB
6. E	6. D	6. B		6. B C	6. EBAFCD
7. B	7. C	7. C		7. A D	or
8. A	8. D	8. A		8. D F	BEAFCD
9. D	9. A D	9. B		9. B C	7. A
10. B	10. B	10. A		10. A F	
11. C D	11. A D	11. A		11. C	
12. B	12. B	12. B		12. B	
13. A D	13. B	13. B		13. A	
14. B	14. B	14. A			
15. B	15. C	15. B			
	16. B	16. A			
	17. A D	17. C			
		18. B			
		19. A			
		20. C			

Drawing conclusions (i)		Drawing conclusions (ii)		
1. E	21. A	1. A	21. C	41. B
2. B E	22. B	2. A	22. A	42. C
3. A	23. A	3. A	23. C	43. B
4. B	24. B	4. B	24. A	44. C
5. B		5. B	25. B	
6. C		6. A	26. A	
7. C		7. A	27. A	
8. B		8. B	28. A	
9. A		9. B	29. B	
10. B		10. A	30. A	
11. A		11. A	31. B	
12. C		12. A	32. B	
13. B		13. B	33. B	
14. C		14. B	34. C	
15. A		15. B	35. A	
16. B		16. B	36. C	
17. A		17. B	37. B	
18. B		18. A	38. C	
19. B		19. B	39. A	
20. A		20. B	40. C	